FULFILLED, NOT FAMOUS

Stories and insights from content creators on building a relationship with your audience, creativity, and perseverance

ELIZABETH M. RATHBURN

NEW DEGREE PRESS

FULFILLED, NOT FAMOUS
Stories and insights from content creators on building a relationship with your audience, creativity, and perseverance

ISBN   978-1-64137-322-7   *Paperback*
        978-1-64137-624-2   *Ebook*

Contents

Introduction

"Whatever you do, do it the way you want to do it and be sure you're having fun doing it...If you get hung up on the idea of trying to go viral...when you're just starting out, all you're gonna do is set yourself up for disappointment."[1] (Nathaniel Wayne, 2019)

* * *

Ever have a creative itch you just didn't know how to scratch?

You know what I'm talking about—that feeling you get when you finish a good book and instantly want to draw the characters; or you see something in a movie like a catalog-perfect living room and want to completely make over your entire home; or you watch a new movie and none of your friends are into it and you want to

---

1   Wayne, Nathaniel in discussion with the author, January 31, 2019.

share your thoughts with someone who cares as much as you do; or you randomly say to your partner one day, "You know, I'd like to learn how to play piano..."

...but you just don't have the time.

Or maybe you do have the time, but don't know how to begin.

Or maybe you know where to begin, but you want to share your creation and don't know how or where.

Believe me, I've been there. For some, myself included, that solution to scratching a creative itch on many levels is YouTube. With over a billion hours watched daily and drawing more eighteen–to-thirty-four-year-old-eyes than network TV, there's a high chance someone will see what you create.[2]

How can you scratch a creative itch with YouTube? Here's one way:

Imagine, just for a minute, turning on your camera, doing a fifteen-minute "geeky ramble" about something pop culture that's on your mind (like a first-thoughts

---

2   "YouTube for Press." YouTube. (August 18, 2019).

reaction of a new trailer or your top ten favorite characters from a show), and uploading to YouTube to an expectant audience who is waiting and ready to view, share, and comment on/discuss the video content. That's a day in the life of Nathaniel Wayne, the creator running the Council of Geeks YouTube channel.

What sets Nathaniel apart from other YouTubers in this book is Council of Geeks is not his full-time job. He has a modest channel of over 36,000 subscribers, which he told me was larger than he ever thought he would get. He doesn't play the analytics game and try to improve his videos for the YouTube algorithm. He doesn't do sponsorships.

He loves his audience and what he does—it's a "reliable outlet" to scratch his creative itch. His conviction that trying to beat the algorithm would suck the fun out of making videos and his humble joy about his great audience of 36,000 subscribers were intriguing.

This seemed to be a different story than what the mainstream says about YouTube and YouTubers. The story is people join YouTube, and other social media platforms, for the chance to get famous quickly; this may be the goal when they start out.

Some make it big. Most don't. Like Nathaniel said, "If all you want to do is become famous, go viral, and have millions of people view you and your content, you will be disappointed."[3]

But what about those people who did not get famous right away but, over time, gained millions of followers? Were there any similarities between Nathaniel and some multimillion subscriber channels? Is it about the clicks or about the content?

Is there such a thing as content for the sake of creative fulfillment anymore?

I wanted to explore this more.

* * *

Thanks to social media, everyone today has the potential to be a celebrity, even if it's just for a day. Social media puts our lives on display, and we post often, becoming little celebrities among our friend groups, waiting for the dopamine hit every time we get a notification someone liked our new photo, and doing crazier and crazier stunts hoping one day we might get invited onto *Ellen*.

---

3   Wayne, Nathaniel in discussion with the author, January 31, 2019.

It is easier than ever to set up a camera (hey, we all have one on our phones now!) and start talking to it. Do makeup. Rant about a new episode of a show. Livestream a video game. People of all ages, including teenagers, are making thousands of dollars a month, just reacting to shows or livestreaming in their bedrooms. That seems so easy! I can pay for college! I'm gonna be famous!

Mom, Dad, I'm gonna be a YouTuber!

The problem is, you can't manufacture a viral video.

You can't predict if your tweet or picture will go viral, and you certainly can't build a loyal following overnight. As you'll see, being a full-time YouTuber is more than just making a lot of money and being invited to exclusive parties, festivals, conventions, and collaborations. It is a lot of hard work, especially if you are doing it all by yourself.

Like with other creative ventures you may pour your soul into, someone, somewhere will appreciate all the work you do to create your final product. I've seen the results of hard work pay off through my extensive history of watching a variety of YouTube channels for many years. I have also experienced it.

YouTube has been a big part of my development as a creative person. I've been watching on and off for over a decade now. I have memories in middle school of looking forward to every Friday's Smosh sketch, in high school counting down to new Starkid musicals, and in college watching *The Philip DeFranco Show* every weekday. And I was subsequently inspired.

I made dumb little vlogs on my crappy laptop webcam—introducing my cats to an invisible audience, going under a pseudonym, and making covers of random musical songs. (Those videos will never see the light of day!) For school projects, when given the opportunity, I opted to make a video. (There's a half-hour version of *Macbeth* floating around out there I'm still proud of!)

For a personal project a couple of years ago, I started the YouTube channel that had been fictional since age twelve: Fantasi Entertainment (#shamelessselfpromotion). It became an outlet for me to try my hand at a few reviews, opinion pieces, and edits which I have slowly added to over time. I have ideas for what I want to do next, but just need the time! (Hmm, now that I've finished writing this book...)

Sometime between then and when I got the opportunity to write a book, I started looking at YouTube differently.

I noticed the plugs for Patreon at the end of every video and paid attention to the types of people I followed, how often they uploaded, and their video lengths. I figured out if making videos was their full-time job and watched countless videos of people talking about the things both they and I loved. Some small channels grew larger while others stayed the same. I saw loyal audience members in the comment sections over and over.

And I realized how different the YouTube of today is from the YouTube of ten years ago...but also how similar it was at its core.

When YouTube began nearly fifteen years ago, when there were no rules, it was just about people experimenting, talking, and exploring the possibilities. It was a brand-new platform, a new way of expressing yourself creatively.

The first YouTubers weren't in it to make money; that wasn't even an option! They were in it to make content. They were becoming creatively fulfilled in a way they might not be in their day jobs.

I believe that is still possible to achieve today, even if YouTube is a full-time job and the creators need to balance making a living and satisfying the audience and sponsors that fund them with finding joy in what they are creating.

YouTube, and the internet at large, is about doing and sharing what you love. It was true decades ago and it is true now. The only difference now is there are more ways than ever before to do this sharing.

Becoming a YouTuber shouldn't be about becoming famous. It should be about doing what you love.

It might be a lot of hard work, but you can ultimately be proud of your output. You get to research a favorite topic, rewatch a favorite show, play a favorite game, or try something new. You get to connect with people all around the world who support you and what you do without ever having met you. And you get to feel creatively fulfilled.

* * *

So you picked up this book. Hi! Who are you?

Are you an aspiring YouTuber (podcaster/livestreamer) looking for advice on how to get started on this fun adventure?

Are you like me and genuinely curious about the new internet culture of having your full-time job be to create content you love supported by an audience who is directly connected to you?

Are you curious about how this whole "making your living from the comfort of your own home" thing works?

Whichever you are or if you're someone else entirely, welcome! I think you'll like what's in here.

The book is divided into three sections. The first gives some basics, like what Patreon is and why the audience is one of your most important tools. The second is origin stories, how some people came up with their channel concepts and how you can too. The third is what happens once you are established, including having a channel as your full-time job and maintaining inspiration, motivation, authenticity, and an audience.

You'll read stories about people who are doing what they love, regardless of whether they are famous. Two brothers are talking about *Harry Potter* and Disney so much they are regarded as experts in those fandoms. One interviewer gives his own spicy twist to the traditional interview-a-celebrity format. A musician uses Google Translate to create gibberish parodies of our favorite pop and musical songs. Academics and musi-cians, hobbyists and comedians, hardcore fans and sim-ple artists all have unique and exciting channel topics, getting-started stories, and hints of advice sprinkled throughout this book.

Some of these YouTubers are famous; I am definitely not one of them. However, all of them, myself included, are fulfilled.

Part I

Basics

I'm going to assume you know what YouTube is.

While I won't give an in-depth history of the platform, I will tell you when it got started (2005), who created it (three former PayPal employees named Jawed Karim, Steve Chen, and Chad Hurley), when people could make money from being YouTubers (May 2007), the first video to reach 1 billion views (the music video for Psy's "Gangnam Style" back in 2012—remember that?), and when I began watching on a somewhat consistent basis (2009).[4]

YouTube has been around for a little while, with plenty of time to rise and fall, learn and grow, and adapt. Some people have been there since the beginning. Others get started every day. It is not the world's only video-sharing online platform, but it is definitely the biggest, with

---

4   Dickey, Megan. "The 22 Key Turning Points in the History of YouTube." *Business Insider.* February 15, 2013.

the most users, sheer number of videos uploaded, and number of advertisers keeping it going. It's also owned by Google as of 2006...that might have something to do with it too.[5]

However, I won't assume you know everything about the ins and outs of running a channel or website, managing a business, interacting with an audience, keeping afloat in the rapidly changing online landscape, or even getting started with taking an idea and turning it into a workable, marketable, consumable format.

I know it's a lot to think about!

But don't worry. I may not know everything about these areas, but by combining the advice of those who have had some experience with my own observations and research, I have put together enough foundation to get you started.

This first section is to put you in the right mindset. I'll be laying out some definitions and concepts that will become vital later on, in the book and in your creative endeavor, including what is so great about the internet, what is Patreon, why taking sponsorships isn't "selling

---

5   Ibid

out" anymore, the importance and possible roles of the audience, and how culture is slowly changing to bring the mainstream to the internet.

Are you excited? I'm excited!

Chapter 1

Don't Forget to be Awesome!

Why would anyone want to make their living through the internet, especially YouTube?

More than once I've gone onto the internet and not liked what I found. So much is dedicated to spreading negativity, even if some of those things are technically newsworthy. I do not feel like my day has improved with this new information. Famous kids do dumb things. This celebrity or that has a scandal. Where was the latest public shooting? The constant bad news, criticism, boycotting of companies or people, manufactured or out-of-proportion drama, and overall unpleasantness does not enrich day-to-day life.

It would be so nice sometimes to just stay away from the internet, but if you're anything like me, you have long since realized it can be pretty difficult to stay away for an extended period. This could be because of your job, many of which rely on the internet in some capacity, or good old-fashioned Fear of Missing Out.

Some people have fully embraced this medium of inter-connectivity and are staking their living on it working for them. That's right—your full-time job can be creating content on YouTube for people you will never meet in person!

Before you dive into creating this content, you should know a little more about the platform. I'll be candid with you and say YouTube isn't scandal-free.

They have rules and guidelines that seem to only apply to certain creators and are ignored for others. They have bots and algorithms scanning for copyrighted material that may hide or block videos and interrupt a channel's growth while the creator was just trying to make an argumentative point by using a piece of copy-righted material under Fair Use guidelines (I will point out it's not all on purpose, since the artificial intelligence behind the algorithms can't always tell the difference between Fair Use and copyright infringement, but it can be frustrating on the creator's side).

They have unspoken preferred partners in certain creators (Hey, everything has a bit of bias! YouTube is still a business.) and will defend them even as other creators call them out on their bias. I'm not pretending it's a perfect platform, but it isn't all a horrible place.

Trust me. And if you don't trust me yet, trust the people who have been around the platform and the internet for a while.

Creator Need-to-Know Definitions:

Algorithm – "A step-by-step procedure for solving a problem or accomplishing some end."[6] The infamous "YouTube algorithm" mentioned throughout the rest of the book is the procedure by which videos and channels are recommended and trending for different users of YouTube, based on not just the subscriptions and viewing history of the user in question, but many other factors not laid out explicitly. The rules are not exact, which is what makes it sometimes difficult to predict how the algorithm will receive a video.

Fair Use – A United States legal doctrine that states under which circumstances you can use copyrighted material without the permission of the copyright holder. There are four factors to consider whether the use of material is fair. YouTube has a detailed article for creators called "What Is Fair Use?" which describes theses four factors, myths about Fair Use, and YouTube's policies.[7] While Fair Use makes it legal to use copyrighted materials in certain circumstances, my advice is to use caution any

---

6   "Algorithm." *Merriam-Webster.* (August 18, 2019).

7   "What is fair use?" *YouTube.* (August 18, 2019).

People who have seen the evolution of the internet and have been creating content for a long time have a more unique perspective on how it can be utilized. Veteran YouTuber, popular online voice, and successful novelist Hank Green still believes the internet can be used for good.

He says, "I believe that it does connect people. It does give people a chance to be more of themselves. It does allow for content to be created for audiences that were being completely ignored and neglected."[8]

This book will hopefully prove this to you if you do not believe it already. The examples of the different You-Tubers and their experiences with their channels and their audiences should paint a picture of the internet being used as a force for good. People can find a community for their niche interests, whether it is traveling, *Star Wars*, or 3D printing. They can find an audience for their crazy ideas. They can be themselves and make connections across the world.

---

8   Ohlheiser, Abby. "It's 2018, and Hank Green still believes the Internet can make the world better." *The Washington Post.* June 24, 2018.

YouTube is a great place to share your thoughts and make these connections, even if you know little about creating videos. It is a skill anyone can learn.

Hank proves you don't have to have gone to school to learn about creating videos and acting and entertainment to create viable content that can influence and teach many people. For example, Hank started out writing a blog called EcoGeek, which was a part of his environmental studies and nonfiction writing college education. This became his full-time job for a while and was his first foray into running an internet business.

In 2007, he and his brother John (yes, *The Fault in Our Stars* John Green) started the Vlogbrothers project, where they traded videos talking about anything to each other as well as the audience. EcoGeek wasn't doing as well during this time, but, as he says, "It was okay because Vlogbrothers was so fun. I sort of believed intrinsically, despite all the evidence, that YouTube was a big deal and I wanted to put all of myself and my energy into this thing."[9]

That is exactly what they did.

---

9   Business Insider. "How Hank Green became one of the Internet's most influential educators." YouTube video, 2:57. Posted [March 2015].

The brothers continued making videos every single day, even if they were on bizarrely unrelated topics, like making up songs or talking about the French Revolution. YouTube eventually approached the Vlogbrothers and offered them money to make next-level content.

They tried to come up with something they were good at doing that was also good for the world. Hank says, "Educational content seemed to be the most logical thing to do, and so we pitched them two ideas: Crash Course and SciShow."[10]

Crash Course is educational content geared toward high schoolers and college students, full of topics like literature, US and world history, and engineering. The history videos, especially the Civil War videos, were a fun addition to my classroom experience while in high school. I enjoyed not just the exciting visuals, but John's humor and delivery, making learning fun.

Hank runs SciShow, which is a more general "science is awesome, the world is fascinating, let's talk about it" approach.[11] The videos seek to expand the viewer's knowledge and satiate their curiosity by getting into the science behind popular science questions and sharing

10   Ibid
11   Ibid

science news. There are several spinoff channels as well, including SciShow Space and SciShow Psych, which are aptly a little more niche in the topics they cover.

In addition to running these educational channels and becoming bestselling novelists, both Hank and John still upload to the Vlogbrothers channel. Back in 2010, they started the annual VidCon, a convention for those who love online video as much as they do.

These YouTube veterans are experts by now at how to navigate the online world, especially YouTube. They have used their platform to spread knowledge and share a little of themselves to millions of fans. The Green brothers absolutely make the internet a brighter place.

Creator Need-to-Know Definition:
Vlog – (as in "Vlogbrothers") Video blog (or more specifically, video web log). As a blog is a written public diary or journal full of thoughts, observations, and opinions of the writer, a vlog incorporates the audiovisual aspects of recording a video with the personal nature of blogs. A person can make a vlog sharing parts of a vacation, walking around a grocery store, or giving their thoughts about a topic in a stationary location.

Hank offers advice to those just starting out: "People will be able to tell if you're having a good time doing this. So make it something that you enjoy doing. You're not just trying to build a YouTube channel. You're also building a skill set. And this will be among the many skill sets that will be important to your life."[12]

Let's look at the first half of that advice: your audience can tell if you're not feeling whatever your content is.

If they're showing up for you and "you" aren't there, they will stop showing up. That is a key part of this current culture of content creators and their audiences. They come for your *content* but stay for *you*. If what you're doing isn't giving you joy anymore, change direction or take a small break to avoid complete burnout.

Your audience will still support you and will understand the need to take a break or try something new. The comment sections aren't just full of trolls anymore (Disclaimer: trolls do still exist in comment sections. Remember what I said about the internet sometimes being a negative place.)

Creator-to-Creator Tip #1
Do something you like—if you're bored, your audience is bored.

---

12   Ohlheiser, Abby. "It's 2018, and Hank Green still believes the Internet can make the world better." *The Washington Post.* June 24, 2018.

Creator Need-to-Know Definition:
Troll – "A person who intentionally antagonizes others online by posting inflammatory, irrelevant, or offensive comments or other disruptive content."[13]

Now let's look at the second half. What is this skill set he is referring to?

Being a YouTuber requires many skills that can be applicable outside of YouTube. These skills include speaking and writing, video and image editing, research, and time management, not to mention the business and finance you need to learn if you become independent and this becomes your full-time job.

You can learn these skills through watching other YouTubers, trial and error, or asking others on the platform for help. These skills are not just beneficial if your dream is to become a full-time YouTuber. They can apply to many situations and areas of life.

YouTube might be a stepping-stone to a dream job, like in entertainment or film, where you can practice script writing or camera angles. It could be a place to hone your hosting or research skills and build a body of work to send to potential employers if you want to be on-cam-

---

13   "Troll." *Merriam-Webster.* (August 18, 2019).

era talent, a blogger or journalist, or even work for a larger YouTube channel or entertainment company.

Outside of general entertainment, you could also showcase research you have done or a talent like music or art for other job opportunities. Any skill you learn while working in the YouTube space is invaluable to anything you do for the rest of your life—especially being able to effectively communicate and express your thoughts.

Creator-to-Creator Tip #2
Continually build and improve upon your skill set.

---

* * *

Hank says, "I believed very early on that online video was a huge, important cultural thing."[14]

YouTube started nearly fifteen years ago, and much has changed. The internet can be a sad place, full of people tearing each other apart, spreading today's worst news, and bringing to light scandals and mistakes some would rather have been left in the dark. But it can also be a place where people can support each other, ideas can be heard, content can be shared, and fandoms can flourish.

---

14   Business Insider. "How Hank Green became one of the Internet's most influential educators." YouTube video, 2:57. Posted [March 2015].

If you're just starting out on YouTube, know you are joining the ranks of some of the smartest, most creative, most selfless people in the world. Take a chance with your first idea. Enjoy yourself, learn something new, and, as the Green brothers will tell you, don't forget to be awesome!

Chapter 2

The Story of Patreon

What is this "Patreon" I've been hearing so much about?

If you're anything like me, you've spent your life hearing repeatedly that if you want to be an artist, you will not make any money. Or, "Find something you like doing, then find someone willing to pay you for it." Or (my least favorite, very misleading, and often sarcastic), "Do what you love, and you'll never work a day in your life!"

Do you see a theme yet?

Yes, the world is screaming at you not to start this little YouTube/other creative endeavor because you won't get any money out of it. But these phrases, often directed at musicians, artists, actors, writers, designers, etc., also make it seem like no correlation exists between doing what makes you happy and earning a livable wage.

I disagree.

YouTube disagreed as well, and in May 2007, it started the YouTube Partner Program.[15] This meant some creators who had a consistent following and audience could apply to join the program. Google advertisements would then appear on their videos, allowing them to earn AdSense.

The thresholds for becoming a partner have changed several times over the years. YouTube has responded to fix problems with partners and advertisers (such as 2017's "Adpocalypse"," when many advertisers pulled all their ads from YouTube or certain channels) with some stricter guidelines and new policies, as businesses should.

However, it seems that unless you are one of the absolute top-performing channels, it is difficult to make your living through just YouTube's AdSense given how much YouTube takes off the top and the variability in the CPM rate. This is even harder for a brand-new creator. Creators were becoming worried. What could they do?

Creator Need-to-Know Definitions:
AdSense – The cut of advertising revenue given to creators as members of the YouTube Partner Program. The important thing to note

---

15   "YouTube elevates most popular users to partners." *YouTube Blog.* May 3, 2007.

> is YouTube/Google will only pay you once you reach $100.[16]
>
> CPM Rate – How much money you can make on YouTube per 1,000 views. This changes depending on the creator, the content of the video, and the advertisers. If CPM is $1, with a 10,000-view video, you would only make $10.[17]

Enter Jack Conte.

Jack Conte is a YouTuber and musician, one of the earliest on the platform starting in 2007. For a while, he was a "self-hating YouTuber," but now he's just a YouTuber... and is also the CEO and founder of one of the most important companies for the modern online entrepreneur: Patreon.

By 2013, Jack felt he was not reaping the full benefits of being monetized on YouTube. He was spending all his money on creating music videos but barely getting any money in return—only a couple hundred dollars in ad revenue each month while consistently getting a million views a month. Jack knew he was not alone in feeling the frustration of being an artist on YouTube trying to make a living doing what you love.

---

16 "How Much do YouTubers Make?—A YouTuber's Pocket Guide [Calculator]." *Influencer Marketing Hub.* May 16, 2019.

17 "How Much do YouTubers Make?—A YouTuber's Pocket Guide [Calculator]." *Influencer Marketing Hub.* May 16, 2019.

One video project in particular pushed him over the edge—the music video for his song "Pedals," released on May 7, 2013. He spent three months making it while maxing out two credit cards and draining his savings account, totaling about $10,000. This video included robots and a replica of the cockpit of the Millennium Falcon. He brought in robotics experts to bring his ideas to life and created the cockpit through his own DIY-ingenuity.

In the behind-the-scenes video, he mentions collapsing in exhaustion at the end of the shoot. He said, "I've given 99 percent before, but this was 100 percent. I had nothing left at the end of this."[18] His fans loved the video, which received over one million views in the first year; it's now up to over two million views.

"It was this rock-bottom moment for me as a creator," he says, referring to giving his all to creating something of value but realizing he would never be paid for it.[19] "It's so demoralizing as an artist to feel so successful, and to have just a discrepancy between the impact you feel you're having on the world and then the paycheck that

---

18   JackConteExtras. "Pedals Behind the Scenes." YouTube video, 9:02. Posted [May 2013].

19   Chaykowski, Kathleen. "Digital Medici: How This Musician-Turned-Entrepreneur Plans To Save Creators From Advertising." *Forbes*. February 13, 2018.

you get at the end of the month[20]...That discrepancy led directly to the formation of Patreon."[21]

In fact, in the first month of uploading the video, Jack made only $54 from YouTube. So, at the end of the "Pedals" music video, he introduced Patreon briefly to his viewers and asked for their help: "Not only am I asking for your help as an artist, but I'm asking for your help bringing this site to life because I think it could be a wonderful thing that could help millions of people."[22]

If only 2013-him knew how widespread this would become for thousands of creators. As of early 2019, Patreon is home to over 100,000 creators supported by over three million patrons! [23]

Patreon is a service where a creator can set up a page and their audience can pay them, either by month or by project. This way, a creator is guaranteed a certain amount of income with everything that they do and

20 Kafka, Peter. "Full transcript: Patreon founder and CEO Jack Conte on Recode Media." *Vox.* August 22, 2017.

21 Chaykowski, Kathleen. "Digital Medici: How This Musician-Turned-Entrepreneur Plans To Save Creators From Advertising." *Forbes.* February 13, 2018.

22 Conte, Jack. "Pedals Music Video (featuring REAL robots)—Conte." YouTube video, 6:08. Posted [May 2013].

23 "Millions and Billions: Celebrating Patrons, Creators, and Major Milestones." *Patreon Blog.* January 23, 2019.

those who give to them, called "patrons," get something in return.

Depending on how much they give in a month, patrons have access to various tiers of rewards, called "perks," all determined by the creator. These perks can include access to works in progress through a service called Lens; extra videos, full-cuts of reaction videos, or bloopers; Patreon-exclusive posts, video chats through Crowdcast, and live chats through Discord; their name listed as a producer at the end of a video; and many other things. Patrons can even have a direct impact on what a channel creates (see Chapter 4 for an example).

Creator-to-Creator Tip #3
While many channels feature links to their Patreon page on their YouTube channel or video descriptions, this is separate from YouTube. For some channels, YouTube has the "membership" feature available, which functions like Patreon, where audience members can give a certain amount in return for perks, but it is much more limited.

Patreon is Jack's way of reviving the idea of becoming a patron of the arts. He says, "It used to be reserved for the wealthy few. It was a privilege to be a patron of the arts. Everyone wants to support and give back, and at the same time, you want some of the stuff. You want the tickets, early access…That's what makes Patreon unique; that's why it's not a fan club."[24]

Patreon takes a small cut of each pledge, 5 percent, and it is significantly less than what YouTube would take, which, according to Jack, is about 45 percent. Since 2013, Patreon has paid out over $1 billion to creators. [25]

Jack doesn't like the word "middleman" to describe how Patreon operates. It is more like another platform, similar to YouTube. It hosts content and interactions and facilitates the transaction of money from audience to creator. But it is up to the creator and the audience to do the rest—creating content, making the audience aware of their Patreon page, and giving out perks as promised in exchange for as little as $1 a month.

Will people get tired of endless Patreon plugs during videos and podcasts?

According to Jack, not for a while. "I've seen the fervor and the excitement around people wanting to pay creators. Sometimes, a creator will say something like, 'I

---

24 Kafka, Peter. "Full transcript: Patreon founder and CEO Jack Conte on Recode Media." *Vox.* August 22, 2017.

25 "Millions and Billions: Celebrating Patrons, Creators, and Major Milestones." *Patreon Blog.* January 23, 2019.

don't want to ask my fans for money,' and my response to that has always been like, 'You don't have to ask them. Literally just let them.' They can't wait to pay."[26]

Patreon is changing the way audience members and creators interact. Audience members see the value in the content they are consuming and, in turn, want to reward the creator for this free entertainment. They are a special subset of an audience, a close-knit group legitimately becoming friends with each other and the creator they support, the ultimate fans in an audience of thousands or millions.

They're more than fans, though. They're *patrons*.

Creator-to-Creator Tip #4
The success of your Patreon comes from your audience. If you have no audience, there is no reason to make a Patreon—that alone is no guarantee you will make money. I will expand on the importance of your audience in Chapter 4.

All I know about Patreon comes from what I hear from other creators—and I will sing its praises several times in the upcoming chapters. I have no firsthand experience; my meager YouTube channel does not fall under the requirements for becoming a YouTube partner, so I

26   Kafka, Peter. "Full transcript: Patreon founder and CEO Jack Conte on Recode Media." *Vox.* August 22, 2017.

don't qualify for AdSense and I don't have a consistent enough audience to warrant using Patreon. But, hypothetically, if I had a few thousand subscribers, and if I did, in fact, want to turn YouTube into my full-time job right this minute, Patreon would be pretty much my only option to make money.

As a creative person (writer, musician, video creator), I can appreciate how much Patreon can help different types of creators, not just YouTubers and podcasters. Everything about Patreon is "creator-first...Everything that we do, every decision that we make, every product that we build, every line of code that we write, we're thinking about it through the lens of 'Is this creator-first? Are we putting creators first?'" [27]

Creators are YouTubers, musicians, graphic designers, cosplayers, painters, podcasters, streamers, filmmakers, crafters, gamers, woodworkers, actors, directors, photographers, writers, designers, and dancers. Creators are people trying to make a living while doing what they love, in direct defiance of most of society. They work very hard, yet they also are fulfilled by what they are doing. Otherwise, they would stop.

---

27   Kafka, Peter. "Full transcript: Patreon founder and CEO Jack Conte on Recode Media." *Vox*. August 22, 2017.

As for the future of Patreon, Jack says, "We want to build something that is meaningful and valuable for creators, that's beneficial to creators because they're underrepresented by tech and the media...I feel like Patreon has the potential to be that seat for the creative class."[28]

Now, Jack is working on creating a balance between running a one-hundred-person company and not giving up on his music. He says, "A lot of creators depend on us being a high-performance team. That's the most important thing in the world to me, so there's less time for music."[29]

But he definitely makes the time for music—he's still a creative person and needs that outlet. While his Jack Conte YouTube channel, where the "Pedals" video lives, has not been updated for years, he still makes music on YouTube as half of the music duo Pomplamoose with his wife Nataly Dawn.

* * *

---

28 Ibid

29 Chaykowski, Kathleen. "Digital Medici: How This Musician-Turned-Entrepreneur Plans To Save Creators From Advertising." *Forbes*. February 13, 2018.

If you are beginning this creative journey, don't forget about the audience-funding platform Patreon! Sign up for an account and consider first becoming a patron of creators you already enjoy, especially those who are doing either a similar project or creating in a similar field. See what they are doing on their Patreon and take some notes. How could you apply similar perks or strategies to your own channel/project? Start small with your perks and reward tiers—you don't want keeping up with your Patreon perks to become your #1 priority; that should always be to create good content you are proud of.

Patreon is an example of not just an option to make money once you get started (Chapter 3 gives some other ways to make money) but also the story of an entrepreneur and innovator who saw a problem and came up with a solution. Jack Conte discovered where he was not being fulfilled and found a way to benefit not just his own experience but those of thousands of others.

Many of the creators mentioned in this book could not do what they are doing without Patreon. On behalf of all creators everywhere, thanks Jack!

Chapter 3

More Monetary Alternatives and Independence

What does it mean to be an independent creator?

There are a few other things to consider about how to make money, including joining a network, remaining independent, and taking sponsorships.

Let's break it down with some examples, shall we?

Comedian Mike Falzone has been on YouTube since 2006, and since then has seen the many changes that have rolled through the website and the online entertainment industry as a whole.

He is operating under the philosophy "that I was going to make a little bit of money in a million different places," which has carried over from his early days as a touring musician.[30] This means he is not just a comedian with regular stand-up shows but also a YouTuber and a podcaster—a content creator ready for anything.

He used to be part of an MCN.

Creator Need-to-Know Definition:
MCN – Multi-channel network. An MCN is a larger entertainment organization that partners with YouTubers and other creators to offer certain services. These services include access to bigger and better sponsors, production and editing facilities, and connections with other creators in the network. In return, just like any contract, the creator must adhere to certain guidelines, including how much of their revenue goes to the MCN or some restrictions on their video content. [31]

Recently, many MCNs have been bought by bigger companies or even had to shut down completely, leaving many creators out in the cold. If they are bought by bigger companies, the creators might have different rules and restrictions on the content they create.

Some more noteworthy MCN acquisitions by larger entertainment companies include AwesomenessTV by DreamWorks Animation in 2013 and Maker Studios

---

30   Falzone, Mike in discussion with the author, January 25, 2019.
31   "What is a YouTube MCN?" *Media Kix.* February 15, 2016.

by Disney in 2014.[32] There was also the bankruptcy of Defy Media in 2018, whose sudden shutdown and lack of communication with their creators created a period of uncertainty as many creators lost several months of income and financial security.

If an MCN shuts down, all the support, monetary or otherwise, the creator would receive dries up. MCNs used to be more popular, but because of the rise of audience funding, more and more creators are stepping away.

Though Mike's experience with them was not bad, it was not the right fit for him. He says, "It just wasn't the best relationship for me...They're kind of used to working with people in a certain capacity but...toward the end of my relationship with those types of people I felt like I could sell myself better, and I was selling myself better than some company who just had me on the backburner could sell me...So I got to the point where I was like, why couldn't I sell ads for myself? Why couldn't I make money for myself? Why are we still working together if you can't sell me? So then we split ways after that."[33]

That's why he likes things like Patreon and the YouTube membership feature, which I briefly mentioned earlier.

---

32 Ibid
33 Falzone, Mike in discussion with the author, January 25, 2019.

He says, "It's the best possible thing."[34] He uses Patreon for the podcast he runs with his wife Zoja (who goes under the name "CoffeeGirl") called *Welcome to Our Podcast*, but he also tests the newer YouTube membership feature, which he has attached to his personal YouTube channel. As mentioned in the previous chapter, this feature functions like Patreon in that there are perks for those who pay, but there is only one option of payment, and channels and creators have to be a YouTube partner and fulfill a few other requirements to activate it. [35]

Mike is still comparing the two. "I go back and forth with them and we see what works and what doesn't work."[36]

In my experience, most creators opt for Patreon because it is much easier to activate (anyone can!) and creators have much more control in setting perks and payment tiers. To me, the Patreon model seems like the more logical route.

I can only speculate the reasons YouTube has not changed their membership feature to be more like Patreon—my guess is there is no competition; Patreon has

34 Ibid

35 Perez, Sarah. "YouTube introduces channel memberships, merchandise and premieres." *Tech Crunch*. June 21, 2018.

36 Falzone, Mike in discussion with the author, January 25, 2019.

that market cornered. As long as people continue to make videos on YouTube and drive traffic to the site itself, the format of the transaction facilitator doesn't matter if the audience wants to pay.

* * *

Patreon and the YouTube membership are a part of this new wave of creativity, the idea that the audience can directly support the creators they enjoy the most. Creators can more easily make a living doing what they love without having to go through MCNs or relying on just YouTube monetization.

As Mike says, "I think it's cool that people obviously get to, maybe in an easier, less roundabout way, make a living from just making stuff. And the people who want to support you could support you without going through too many avenues, without too many people having their fingers in the pot."[37]

It has taken this long, from the start of the Partner Program and popularity of MCNs, for there to be a straightforward way for creators to make money. In the past, especially with MCNs, it was very difficult for

---

37   Falzone, Mike in discussion with the author, January 25, 2019.

creators to receive the money they were making. There were too many people to go through.

But that has changed. Mike says, "And I think that's cool because it gets muddied and it gets messy and convoluted. So the more direct you can make it, the better, for sure."[38]

Creator-to-Creator Tip #5

While it is a good thing there are more people than ever on YouTube in terms of the chances of getting eyes on your content, there is also a disadvantage.

Mike says, "The way it was explained to me by someone who worked at YouTube was [YouTube] used to be like a town, and so it's easy to get recognized in your town. You do good work, and then the town talks about it. And then it became a city...and now it's a world. There's a lot of people on the website but it's significantly harder to break through."[39]

But that doesn't mean you shouldn't try if this is what you want to do.

Mike absolutely embodies the spirit of fulfilled, not famous. He wants to keep making content and stay in touch with his audience—which now pulls fans from many different spaces and different eras of his channel and work: his music, podcasts, vlogs, and hosting on other channels.

---

38 Ibid
39 Ibid

But in the end, he says, "I just kind of do it to make good stuff. I don't like playing the game so much, and I think that's the reason why I'm maybe not as popular as some other people...I have a make good stuff first mentality and though it may not be the most popular stuff, I just try to be good...No matter what it is, YouTube or music or whatever, you've gotta make a good thing first...At the end of the day, it's still making a funny video for people to enjoy, so you can't lose track of that."[40]

Creator-to-Creator Tip #6
Make good stuff first.

You could argue it's not true independence if you are getting support from your audience, but as long as you own your content, you are independent—in other words, a larger company like an MCN does not own everything you put on your channel.

What can happen if there are too many people involved? I know from experience it is easy for a creative vision to be stifled. More people involved means more people to please. If other people own, or have a stake in, your content, they can dictate what you can and cannot say. It's all a game of give and take—how much are you will-

---

40   Falzone, Mike in discussion with the author, January 25, 2019.

ing to exchange for money? So some choose to remain independent.

How do sponsorships fit into all of this? Any time something controversial shows up in the news based on the actions of a person or a group of people, you always hear about their sponsors and different brand deals. Often, sponsors rescind their support of a particular event or discontinue showing advertisements featuring a particular athlete.

You do have to consider sponsors when creating. Sponsors do not own your content, but as they are businesses in and of themselves, they can choose to end their relationship with you. You don't have to bend over backwards to cater to them—just be aware of their general guidelines.

A stigma or skepticism exists surrounding sponsorships. People think since someone is paid to talk about the product, it might not be that good. But not every experience with sponsorships should be seen as "selling out." Some sponsors like to work with the creators they sponsor, so both parties have an enjoyable exchange.

Let me show you what I mean.

* * *

Matt Cremona is one of many YouTubers who makes their living sharing their projects and processes through YouTube. He is a woodworker, best known for his weekly shop updates and showing all steps of his project creation, from the log the wood comes from to the final product. He has been a full-time YouTuber since the winter of 2015 and enjoys sharing his projects with his audience.

Like many YouTubers, Matt has several sponsors. One of his main, recurring sponsors is Triton Tools, a power tool company. That makes sense—a power tool company sponsoring a woodworker. He says, "They've been great to work with. They've sent me on a lot of trips."[41]

What seemed to be a little less conventional was a trip they sent Matt on in 2017.

In a six-day chair-making course in the UK, the participants learned how to make a chair using just hand tools. Matt made a video documenting his process and uploaded it to the Triton Tools channel. [42] But he also

41 Cremona, Matt in discussion with the author, January 21, 2019.
42 Triton Tools. "Matt Cremona making a Windsor chair from fresh logs." YouTube video, 14:59. Posted [October 2017].

shared with his own audience the results of the course and his plans to finish the chair in the future. He then used his channel to drive his audience to the Triton video for a bit of mutual cross-promoting.

So why would a power tool company send one of their "brand champions" across the pond to make a video about hand tools?

Matt thinks "they just wanted to be able to share a cool story, something I did that my audience would enjoy...a lot of companies out there are kind of getting into this space and finally realizing that it's an actual thing that actually can provide value."[43]

He likes working with them because they don't tell him to "jam our products down people's throats," which is what some sponsorships turn into. Instead, Triton essentially told him, "we just want to be part of the experience."[44]

* * *

Sponsorships are not the only way to make money on YouTube, of course. I've mentioned YouTube's AdSense

---

43 Cremona, Matt in discussion with the author, January 21, 2019.
44 Ibid

and memberships, and Patreon, but there are other donation services like PayPal audience members can use to support their favorite creators—a straight-up, one time, "'let me give you some money because I believe in what you are doing" kind of gift.

Another thing Matt does is "the paid content route. [I] put together classes and instructional content that people could buy...which I started doing in 2016...I do two of those [projects] a year, one summer, one winter."[45]

Creator-to-Creator Tip #7

As other ways of making money, many YouTubers write books, both fiction and nonfiction, expressing themselves creatively by sharing their experiences in essays or writing about something else altogether (I've already mentioned the Green brothers). Musicians may also sell their recordings, albums, or arrangements.

There is also the ever-popular merchandising of a creator's brand. Many creators sell merchandise (often shortened to just "merch") that can range from anything to t-shirts and hats to buttons and stickers. These usually feature the logo or name of the creator as well as inside jokes and references to the content itself for fans who may be strangers in real life to identify each other.

For reliable support, having a good sponsor is the best solution for some creators. However, getting the right

---

45 Ibid

sponsor for the video and the channel audience can be tricky sometimes.

Often, sponsors go to the creators instead of the other way around. They see the kind of content the creator is making and determine if the creator would be a good fit for their product or service. The creator can then determine if they want to associate themselves with this product or service and accept or reject the sponsorship. They might try it out first if they are not using it already.

The world of sponsorships and advertising online is changing, especially when compared to the early days of being a YouTuber. Matt recalls approaching companies in the early days, offering them advertising space on his videos and them essentially laughing him off. His response was, "Okay. Keep running your print ads. That's fine."[46]

Stay stuck in the Dark Ages because the internet moves fast.

In my "expert" opinion (I was a communication major), print advertisements are not your best bet in most cir-

_____

46   Cremona, Matt in discussion with the author, January 21, 2019.

cumstances. That's a tip not just for creators but for any business.

Because this world is changing, a much more harmonious relationship can exist between creator and sponsor. Like with Matt and Triton Tools, a sponsor can support a channel and the creator can incorporate the sponsor into their regular content as they wish.

Sponsors should now see the benefits of letting the creator incorporate the product or do their own twist on some copy sent by the sponsor. The relationship between sponsor and creator should not be static. It can be very dynamic, and, as Matt's experience shows, fun. Sponsors are getting smarter.

Another benefit to having sponsors is the creator can still technically call themselves independent; they just need to be sure to incorporate the sponsor as their contract indicates.

Sometimes having a sponsor is the only way to survive as an independent creator, and if the relationship between sponsor and creator is good, and beneficial for both, why not do it?

Being an independent creator has given Matt the freedom to pursue what he wants to create. He became a full-time YouTuber "because that seems like that would be a lot more rewarding and a lot more of an interesting path for me in life than sitting at a desk—which I still do a lot of. I don't sit at a desk for someone else, I sit at my own desk for my own stuff."[47]

Creator-to-Creator Tip #8
On being a YouTuber, Matt says, "If someone says it's easy, they're lying to you." But "it's incredibly rewarding and fun and I couldn't imagine doing anything else."[48]

* * *

Both stories give a new creator even more options to consider when thinking about starting a creative endeavor and eventually turning it into a living. MCNs work for some creators but not all. Independence is more common than ever thanks to ways creators can earn a living, own their content, and make what they want to make.

---

47 Cremona, Matt in discussion with the author, January 21, 2019.
48 Ibid

Chapter 4

Audience Participation and the Power of Community

What is the single most important tool you'll have in your "life as a creator" toolbox?

If you looked at the chapter title, you've probably figured it out—it's the audience.

As a student of communication, I know that the audience can make or break any message. Without an audience, there is no communication. The message gets lost in the void, and the creator gets no feedback. Without understanding the audience, the message might appear muddled.

For example, you might create something you think most of your audience will enjoy but only a certain, smaller portion (called a *segment*) does. Worst-case scenario, you've just lost your general audience.

> **Creator Need-to-Know Definition:**
> Segment—In the marketing sense, dividing and targeting part of an audience based on similarities—for instance, demographics like age, gender, and location or psychographics like attitudes and interests.

Do you need the audience to be fulfilled? Well, no, I suppose not. There is such a thing as creating something for yourself.

But if you're putting your work online, chances are you want someone to see it. You need your audience, not just for the possible monetary support via Patreon but also for the interaction, feedback, and shared experiences.

You might not believe me (maybe you've had a bad experience with trolls in the past—it's up to you how much you want to ignore them or straight-up erase comments) so I'll share with you two channels that use their audiences to benefit the channel as a whole.

Audience as Active Participants in Channel Content

Dominic Smith, on a channel recently rebranded as Dominic Noble, is a YouTuber quite familiar with including the audience in creating his content.

This content, mainly film reviews and a book-to-film adaptation series called *Lost in Adaptation*, draws in an audience who are fans of not just the subjects of the videos, but also Dom's own style, camera presence, and opinions.

His rapid-fire way of speaking, the occasional characters he plays, how he is not afraid to hold back opinions, and the consistent structure of the videos suck you in and keep you hooked. I once binged all his Book 1/Season 1 *Game of Thrones* videos in an afternoon!

Pop Culture Plug

Game of Thrones is an HBO series running eight seasons between 2011 and 2019. It is a fantasy show based on George R. R. Martin's currently unfinished book series entitled *A Song of Ice and Fire*, of which the first book is *A Game of Thrones*. One of the most-viewed and highest-awarded television shows of all time, while airing, it was a readily available source of conversation and content for many creators who expressed their love of the show through reviews, book-to-show comparisons, and music parodies, among other things.

With all the different books and films out there, the amount of work that goes into making a single video, and the desire to have a successful video after all that work, how does he choose what to do next?

Simple. Sometimes, he just goes to the audience, whom he calls his "Beautiful Watchers."

Specifically, he goes to his Patreon.

On Patreon, some of his higher tiers allow for patrons to choose an adaptation for Dom to review, or an atypical adaptation review that is not simply book-to-film (like adaptations involving video games, plays or musicals, or TV shows).

Patrons also can get early access to videos, participate in surveys that show up during the videos stating whether they read the book or watched the film, and share opinions of upcoming video topics.

Dom is a huge fan of Patreon and has found it to be "an absolute godsend," especially "for the little guy."[49] At about 150,000 subscribers, without Patreon, it would

---

49   Smith, Dominic in discussion with the author, January 28, 2019.

have been impossible for Dom to turn YouTube into his full-time job.

This is because he does not have to just rely on YouTube's monetization (which benefits mainly bigger channels) or sponsorships (of which he has only Amazon's Audible, chosen because of the extreme relevance to the channel) for income.

As a creator posting early videos and other updates on Patreon, he says, "It's nice to get instantaneous feedback for anything you do...you pretty much get instant gratification for putting the work in."[50]

Outside of Patreon, Dom finds some familiar faces in the people who regularly stay and comment. Since he does everything related to the channel, including research, filming, and editing, by himself, it is just not feasible to connect with every single commenter. That's just a fact when you get hundreds or thousands of comments.

But there have been a few instances where he has made a connection outside of Patreon.

---

50 Ibid

For example, after he reviewed the *Fifty Shades* books and films, some members of his audience approached him and said "they were survivors of abuse. And that my videos helped them realize this and get out of the relationship, so that was huge for me. That was deeply moving to find out that these stupid videos I had made had had that big of an effect on someone's life...I've met a few people at conventions and stuff although a lot of people have contacted me over email...to share stories like that. That's always deeply appreciative when they do."[51]

> **Creator-to-Creator Tip #9**
> If you like instant gratification or feedback, Patreon is a good place to release content as soon as you are finished.

As for the future of the channel, Dom is content to just keep doing what he's been doing. He has found content he enjoys making with an audience that keeps coming back.

He says, "I know a lot of my fellow creators are using this as a stepping-stone to something bigger like they want to go into mainstream filmmaking or writing or being journalists or something. I'm unusual among my

---

51 Smith, Dominic in discussion with the author, January 28, 2019.

friend group in that this was my aspiration. I really did want to be a YouTuber, and this is where I wanted to be and where I want to stay so I'm more nervous than them because if this goes under, then that's my dream gone. I don't want to not follow it just because it looks like it might disappear someday."[52]

Will YouTube ever disappear? Dom thinks it's hard to say "because we're sort of in uncharted territory, business-wise...nothing lasts forever...I'm just hoping to get a good run out of this before it all changes."[53]

With YouTube's monopoly as the main video sharing platform and Patreon as a supportive tool for the creative entrepreneurs of today, the internet is settling into a bit of a groove in allowing people to make a living through videos.

But as Dom said, nothing lasts forever. Just because this groove is becoming familiar does not mean it will stay that way. Something could overtake YouTube or dethrone Google. If the internet has taught us anything, it is that the status quo can be changed in an instant.

---

52 Ibid
53 Ibid

That doesn't seem likely right now, not with loyal audiences eager for content and consistently supporting creators.

Until something else takes over as the next big video sharing platform (if that ever happens), Dom and his audience will stay right where they are, maintaining a positive relationship between creator and audience, with a creator open and willing to get to know his audience and an audience that not only supports the creator and gets basic video and chat access but is also part of the creative process. This will keep them much more invested in the content in the years to come, no matter where the videos live.

So that's a story of how the audience can directly impact the content on a channel and how to use Patreon to your advantage. But what if you want to go a step further and instead of helping just your channel, you did something good for the larger community?

Audience as Members of a Larger Community

Chris Christian is one of the lucky YouTubers who turned an obsession into a living. This obsession was *Game of Thrones* on his channel, Smokescreen. As he quickly found out after starting, there is a community of *Game of Thrones* YouTubers and an audience eager for any kind of content relating to the show and the books it was based on.

According to Chris, the *Game of Thrones* community, on YouTube especially, is "a tight-knit community, it really is. And the support is sometimes overwhelming and unbelievable."[54]

There are many perks to creating a channel that follows a show airing new episodes. For one thing, there is new material to base your content on every week for as long as the season goes.

While that can box you in a bit—when you're in a season, "everything's so time sensitive"[55]—it still guarantees a certain amount of traffic (especially when the show you're talking about is one of the biggest ever created, in the case of *Game of Thrones*, or when any show has a vocal and dedicated audience, which is the case of pretty much any show). Many more ears are ready to listen to opinions about the previous episode and theories about the upcoming episode and drop in their two cents while they are at it.

---

54   Christian, Chris in discussion with the author, January 21, 2019.

55   Ibid

Many YouTubers, like Chris, enjoy interacting with their audiences through the comment section, looking through their different ideas and replying to as many as they can.

He says, "That's one thing I focused on the first year or two...I replied to every single comment. Now it's almost impossible but...I've got a lot of people that said they subscribed just because I interacted with them."[56]

Creator-to-Creator Tip #10
When you get hundreds or thousands of comments, it can be time-consuming to go through all of them. But taking some time, maybe even setting a time limit, and replying to some comments can go a long way to show your audience just how much you care.

How can a content creator take audience interaction to the next level?

On YouTube, this instantaneous connection with an audience can occur through a livestream. But Chris took this a step further. He took advantage of the fact his audience liked interacting with him between Seasons 6 and 7 of *Game of Thrones*. He says, "I didn't enjoy

---

56 Christian, Chris in discussion with the author, January 21, 2019.

the post-show that HBO ran, and a lot of people seemed to echo that sentiment."[57]

Thus, 10:30 livestreams on Smokescreen's channel on Sunday nights became an option for *Game of Thrones* fans, even when the show was not airing. He says, "We started doing that way before Season 7, consistently, and then all of a sudden during Season 7 we'd have five thousand viewers."[58]

Then, Chris had an idea.

"I [was] able to use that opportunity for the...season finale last year to do a charity stream for St. Jude."[59] This was for the Season 7 finale, and while Chris and the chat discussed the episode, there was also a live counter of how much was raised. Viewers knew about the charity aspect in advance.

The stream aired on August 27, 2017, and as of this writing, the recorded stream has over 125,000 views (hovering around three thousand through a majority of

---

57 Ibid
58 Ibid
59 Ibid

the actual stream).[60] "We raised $8,000 in three hours, and I thought that was pretty damn cool."[61]

Chris is right. That is pretty damn cool, not just in terms of charity but considering all that had to fall into place to raise a significant portion of money.

And money was raised: $8,015 to be precise. I did my research![62]

That's a lot of money, especially for a relatively small YouTube channel. And what is so impressive is within twenty minutes of the stream starting, the original goal of $2,000 was met. Chris had to keep raising the goal because more people kept donating.

Chris took into account the modern idea of time shifting—as much as we may like certain shows, we want to watch them in our own time (you know, on-demand television and channel streaming apps).

This stream was over four hours long, which ran into the early hours of Monday morning, and for many peo-

60 SmokeScreen. "Game of Thrones Season 7 Episode 7 Finale Review / Reaction—Live Charity Show!" YouTube video, 4:03:26. Posted [August 2017].
61 Christian, Chris in discussion with the author, January 21, 2019.
62 "Support St. Jude Children's Hospital!" *Tiltify*. (August 19, 2019).

ple, that might not have been practical. So if the rest of the viewers, approximately 122,000 of them, watched or listened to the stream at some other time, they could still donate. While the stream happened on Sunday night, he left the link to donate live until Thursday.

Creator Need-to-Know Definitions:

Livestream – A live video feed from a particular channel where the audience can directly interact with the creator through a chat feature. YouTube channels have had the ability to livestream since summer 2016. Since then, YouTube has been updating and fine-tuning the creator livestreams to make them more creator and audience friendly.[63]

Super Chat – A newer feature of YouTube livestream chatting. Viewers can pay a certain amount of money and essentially "tip" the streamer. This tip is called a Super Chat. The viewer's question or comment gets pinned to the top of the chat, and the more they pay, the longer it is pinned.[64] This is another way for creators to make a little money while viewers, maybe even those who are not on Patreon, can give a little back.

Twitch – A social media platform dedicated entirely to livestreaming, first created in 2004 and described as a place where people could stream their lives à la *Big Brother*.[65] Just like with YouTube and podcasting, Twitch streamers can monetize their content as a Twitch affiliate

63   "We'll do it live—a new chapter in YouTube's live stream." *YouTube Creator Blog*. June 23, 2016.

64   Garun, Natt. "YouTube launches Super Chat, a tool that lets you pay to pin comments on live streams." *The Verge*. January 12, 2017.

65   Cook, James. "Twitch founder: we turned a 'terrible idea' into a billion-dollar company." *Business Insider*. October 20, 2014.

or a Twitch partner.[66] Though it is not the only site with the ability to livestream, Twitch has a major focus on community and creating a fun experience for both the streamers and users.

So how did this all come together? It did not just happen overnight, and it took some smart thinking and understanding of not just the platform, but the audience.

- Chris had to establish the pattern of a weekly livestream, on the same day at the same time.
- This had to happen well enough in advance so it was consistent before Season 7 of *Game of Thrones*.
- Subscribers and non-subscribers had to find out about the livestreams, either through following Smokescreen or seeing it through YouTube recommended (which the YouTube algorithm would like if this content was relevant to their interests).
- The following had to be consistent enough for Chris to make the livestream for charity, so there was a good chance more money could be raised.
- He had to add a time-shifting option for the rest of the consistent, non-live viewers.

There you have it—one example of how to use your platform to do something good.

---

66 Mior, Lisa. "The past, present and future of Twitch: an interview with Chase from Twitch.tv." *CG Mag Online*. September 7, 2018.

Chris reflected on how all this came together. He says, "It was really really good to be able to use the platform and the success of the show...and the community and do something good."[67]

That's right—fandom isn't just about fighting about which characters should be in relationships and coming up with the craziest theories of what could happen next.

It's about the power of a community, backing an idea, supporting an endeavor or a person.

It doesn't matter if a channel has 10 million, 1 million, 100,000, or 10,000 subscribers. Every channel has the potential to become a community that can be a force for good. There's also the added bonus when a majority of content is coming from the most popular show on at the moment: a built-in group of die-hard fans who want to talk about this thing they enjoy watching.

Of course, that didn't last forever.

Season 8 was the end of the show, and all the *Game of Thrones* YouTubers will need to decide (or have already started working toward) their new channel focus now

---

67   Christian, Chris in discussion with the author, January 21, 2019.

that the reliable supply of new source material has ended.

Chris has some ideas: "'Nobody's ever said [Smoke-screen] was *Game of Thrones*. It's an entertainment channel. At some point, I just have to make sure that people understand that this is my thing, and there will be other content. It's not just that show."[68]

For one awesome night, that community put their gathering to good use. What an example to set for others on the platform!

Creator-to-Creator Tip #11
Chris discovered that an audience will "follow you anywhere...and they'll watch you or listen to you talk about anything."[69] You just need to earn it.

As an example of how long it takes to write a book, between our interview and my final draft, Season 8 of *Game of Thrones* was anticipated, aired, and finished. Let this be an example for the creators reading this—no matter what you want to create, it is certainly not going to happen overnight.

* * *

---

68 Christian, Chris in discussion with the author, January 21, 2019.
69 Ibid

The audience is the most important tool in your creator toolbox. It is not just there so you have someone to share your content with. Your audience can become participants in helping you decide what to create for your channel, like for Dominic Noble, or they can join you as a member of a larger community to raise money for or spread awareness of a good cause. They are there to support you, and today more than ever, audience members enjoy feeling closer to the creators and being part of the creative process.

There is no communication without an audience. They can support you, give you ideas, and help you achieve your goals. And you can give right back, becoming so much more than a source of entertainment or a giver of Patreon rewards.

Respect your audience, use your audience, know your audience.

Chapter 5

Bringing Celebrities to YouTube

How does mainstream entertainment interact with YouTube?

If you have picked up this book with little understanding of making a living entertaining others on YouTube, you might be wondering what your favorite celebrities from other divisions of entertainment (film, music, etc.) think about YouTube and how they might interact with it.

Here is one way many of your favorite celebrities have made their way onto YouTube...combined with very hot chicken wings.

Welcome to *Hot Ones*, the show hosted by Sean Evans on the YouTube channel First We Feast.

The premise? It's your standard interview-a-celebrity show, but as the interview goes on, both the guest and Sean eat increasingly hotter chicken wings.

This can lead to some interesting results. *Hot Ones* started in 2015 but took off after the extremely entertaining episode with popular comedians Keegan-Michael Key and Jordan Peele (AKA Key & Peele) went viral in 2016.

Sean felt from the beginning it would be a success. During an early episode with Machine Gun Kelly, he remembers, "While it's happening, there are times when I was like, 'this is good internet.'[70] He was getting up, he's walking around the room, he's screaming, he's so uncomfortable, but it's theatrical and amazing on this black background nothing set. It was just explosive energy. And when that was going on, that's when I knew this show is different. This show is special. This show is something the world needs now."[71]

Keep his last point in mind as we move into Part II and explore different ways to come up with your premise. Does the world need your creation?

---

70 BUILD Series. "Sean Evans Speaks On His Show "Hot Ones"." YouTube video, 22:08. Posted [June 2017].

71 Smith, Dave. "Inside the hottest show on YouTube, where celebrities answer questions while eating blazing hot wings." *Business Insider.* November 29, 2017.

Hot Ones is like everyone's favorite late-night talk shows, but slightly different. It doesn't feel rehearsed, and there is no studio audience. The show takes a format we already know so well and changes it to fit the You-Tube format. It has something new every week, with celebrities in different industries (including music, film, television, sports, online, and more).

Does the world need this right now?

Sure.

I think the raw reactions Sean gets from adding the hot sauce and making his guests uncomfortable (because of the extreme spiciness, not because of the questions) brings the guests closer to the average audience member's level.

That's what makes it so intriguing, and popular, and some people need to see this. I personally enjoy the interview aspect more, but each person has their own tastes (pun intended).

So consider this when thinking about what you are about to create. Whatever it may be, how will it affect the world? If it grew to an audience of a few million, what kind of impact could it have? If the answer is just "entertain people," that's definitely okay! That is what most entertainment sets out to do anyway.

Creator-to-Creator Tip #12
Consider what the impact of your content could be. Will it inspire a movement? Breathe life into a dead fandom? Just make people happy?

Like I mentioned in my introduction, while there is no way to predict if and how you will go viral, that possibility always exists. It could be the right guest at the right time.

One of the biggest names early on was Kevin Hart in 2016, which Sean also contributes to the success of the show. He says, "The way the Kevin Hart thing came together was kind of crazy because he's such a big star, but he was shooting Jumanji in Hawaii and wanted to do this show. His team flew us out and put us up and all that stuff for the show."[72]

The fact that Hart's team saw potential in doing this show and celebrities want to do it keeps it going.

This speaks to some of the changes we are seeing overall with how celebrities are interacting in the digital space.

---

72 BUILD Series. "Sean Evans Speaks On His Show "Hot Ones"." YouTube video, 22:08. Posted [June 2017].

They began to see it as a viable option to reach a potential audience. *Hot Ones* combines this idea of being able to go viral with the fact that some people like watching other people suffer...in a funny way.

Sean says, "I think we're a good show if you want to put highly targeted eyeballs on your project because people are into the drama, that sort of wing over wing, watching them melt down thing. It's painful and it sucks, but on sort of a pound-for-pound basis, you're gonna get a real stretch out of it because it is popular."[73]

He has also noticed this trend of celebrities wanting to get into the online world. It is where entertainment is heading, and *Hot Ones* is just one example.

He says, "People do talk about it. Increasingly, celebs are finding that in the YouTube space, in the digital space, they can extend a little bit more. The late-night shows don't have the punch that they used to have. So now there are these upstart franchises and shows that bubble up online, and now it's just not even a bad play if you're gonna do press."[74]

---

73 BUILD Series. "Sean Evans Speaks On His Show "Hot Ones"." YouTube video, 22:08. Posted [June 2017].

74 Ibid

So why not go to a studio, answer some questions, and eat some chicken? Your name alone will bring in the views, whether it is on a smaller entertainment channel looking for interviews for your upcoming film or an established show like *Hot Ones* where the premise is well-known.

Creator-to-Creator Tip #13

While talking to fellow YouTuber Philip DeFranco, Sean reflected, "We're very fortunate in that the success that we have, we're creatively fulfilled by it. And then the failures that we have, it's the same exact way. I'm not necessarily working and doing something for other people and not feeling interested or emotionally involved. That, to me, is what I hold on to and treasure most."[75]

Sean makes it clear that what matters to him and his team is the interview itself. He says, "To us, we're an interview show, and that's the oldest construct in the history of media. We don't feel like we're some sort of gimmick; what we feel like we've done is taken the interview and turned it on its head."[76]

---

75   DeFranco, Philip. "A Conversation With Ep 2—Sean Evans Reveals How He Truly Feels About Hot Ones, Kevin Hart, & More!" YouTube video, 56:37. Posted [April 2018].

76   Smith, Dave. "Inside the hottest show on YouTube, where celebrities answer questions while eating blazing hot wings." *Business Insider.* November 29, 2017.

And they very much take the research of the interviews seriously.

He says, "When it comes to the interview questions, how we game plan it, it's just what it looks like. We read and watch every single thing that we can."[77] Sean does this part by dividing and conquering with the producer of *Hot Ones*, Chris Schonberger.

The process is similar depending on the guest—watch as many YouTube videos featuring the guest as possible, listen to all their music if they're a musician, read their book if they just wrote a book.

"I think it's by virtue of caring that we set ourselves apart because there's so much in media that's just making the donuts dance, and we knew if we could differentiate, which just means rolling your sleeves up and getting after it, we knew we'd have a real viable property."[78]

This adds to their success and appeal to a wider audience. They are not just another interview show, and they are not just the "show with the hot wings." They

77 Ibid

78 Smith, Dave. "Inside the hottest show on YouTube, where celebrities answer questions while eating blazing hot wings." *Business Insider*. November 29, 2017.

take the time to put in the research to ask the best questions to get the best show.

What matters is the interview, and even more important is the focus on the guest. For example, in the Jonas Brothers episode, one of the first questions Sean asks Nick was about when Nick spent a week training with the Los Angeles Dodgers in 2010. Nick was excited to respond because not many people ask about it. [79]

An interesting distinction between *Hot Ones* and other YouTube shows is the idea that the focus of the video is not on Sean, but on whoever his guest is.

"I feel like with the show it's so stripped down, it's a black background, it's the wings, it's the sauce, and it's a bald guy. So if it's the Sean Show all the time, eventually maybe people get sick of that or they don't vibe with me. I think the key for us is whoever is in that seat, we're going to carefully shape this interview around them. We're gonna make them the star of the show because that way you have a different viewer experience every single time, and that's why we're drawing from such a wide array of

79 First We Feast. "The Jonas Brothers Burn Up While Eating Spicy Wings | Hot Ones." YouTube video, 27:30. Posted [May 2019].

people. We want the viewer experience to complement the personality of whoever is sitting in that seat."[80]

And this also sets this show apart from late-night shows as well, where the personality of the host is more often than not what draws people in to watch. Here, it is all about the guest.

* * *

Why is *Hot Ones* important in this YouTube conversation? It is bringing celebrities, core members of the mainstream entertainment world, onto YouTube. One challenge facing YouTubers, and any kind of online entrepreneur is not being taken seriously by "the mainstream."

However, through shows like *Hot Ones*, the mainstream television/film/music/celebrity/entertainment world can see that online entrepreneurs are just as relevant in creating content and marketing possibilities. They are just as serious in what they create and have audiences of their own.

80 DeFranco, Philip. "A Conversation With Ep 2—Sean Evans Reveals How He Truly Feels About Hot Ones, Kevin Hart, & More!" YouTube video, 56:37. Posted [April 2018].

If you are looking to get a celebrity on your channel or podcast, it will take some work (and maybe a little luck). There is no surefire way to get their attention, but using your online network, including your audience and fellow creators, as well as social media to make contact are good places to start. It may also depend on the celebrity you are trying to reach. Perhaps someone well-known in your area of interest has an accessible email address. Businesspeople might be easier to reach than A-list Hollywood actors.

Some YouTube channels or Twitch streamers are getting more views than broadcast television—remember, YouTube has more eighteen-to-thirty-four-year-old eyes watching it than network television. Certain YouTubers have the money, the house, the car, the following to be considered celebrities in the traditional sense, up there with movie stars and musicians. The definition of celebrity is changing to accommodate this new generation of those made famous through their internet creations.

Hot Ones is helping pave the way for a new kind of acknowledgment and respect for non-traditional creators, one wing at a time.

Part II

Channel Concepts

I hope you have a better understanding of some of the "behind-the-scenes" of being online.

I understand there might be a lot to keep track of and starting as a business right away may seem a bit overwhelming. That's fine.

If that's the case for you, take a step back and start by doing it as something extra, not quite a full-time job. No one says you have to do that right away. Do whatever you can easily do, whether it is every week or every month—whatever it takes to fulfill you. Keep it fun; you should want to do this!

As you get more into the rhythm of creating videos and new skills you've picked up become easier, you could start creating more videos more often. Eventually, you might have a good-sized audience and enough Patreon supporters to feel comfortable making this your full-time job.

But we're getting ahead of ourselves here.

Now that you know more about running a creative endeavor online, you still might not have a solid idea of what your concept will be. Are you a musician who enjoys watching basketball? The biggest nerd in your friend group? A knitter? Conspiracy theorist? Activist?

What could you possibly make a channel about?

That's where I, and other YouTubers, come in. This next section is to get you thinking about your concept. You can go about this in several ways to ensure you are doing something you will enjoy and/or be challenged by. Either way, the result is to give you an idea that might scratch that creative itch and get you creatively fulfilled.

I recommend taking notes and brainstorming after you read each chapter, especially if one method in particular jumps out at you. If you are already sure you have a solid channel/concept idea, you still might learn something about life after a channel concept through a few more YouTube origin stories and sprinkles of advice.

Keep your mind open and get those creative juices flowing!

Chapter 6

Just Have Fun!

How can I work on this project with a partner?

If you're not sure where to begin when starting a creative endeavor, why not find someone to share it with?

Having a partner to bounce ideas off of and share both the workload and the limelight might make starting something new a little less daunting and a little more fun. And if you're friends, well, that chemistry should be tangible right through the screen, drawing viewers in.

But is it possible to make your living just laughing with your best friend?

Rhett McLaughlin and Link Neal, a pair of YouTubers known as Rhett & Link, are doing just that, turning years of making videos together into a company united behind the idea of "mythicality." This concept is so big they wrote an entire book about it. Basically, it is a combination of curiosity, creativity, and tomfoolery. Rhett says, "We want everything that we do to have that value," meaning mythicality.[81]

It's up to the audience to judge how well they apply these concepts to their work, but their sheer number of subscribers seems to indicate they are doing something right.

Their most successful content is their daily morning talk show called *Good Mythical Morning*, with over fifteen hundred episodes to date on a channel with over fifteen million subscribers and consistently over a million views per episode. You might think doing a show with the same person each weekday for a few years might have a breaking point, a moment when the magic will end and they will run out of ideas.

That has not happened yet.

Rhett & Link have been friends since first grade and started making videos together when they were teenagers and in high school, long before YouTube was a thing. They hosted these videos on their own website

---

81   Ifeanyi, KC. "Inside The "Mythical" Minds And Digital Empire Of YouTube Pioneers Rhett & Link." *Fast Company*. March 29, 2017.

and just had a goal of creating things together, with no particular direction in mind.

That changed in 2006 when someone put one of their videos on YouTube.

Rhett says, "It got more views than that particular video had gotten on our website. We thought maybe there's something to this YouTube thing. And that started the whole online thing, and that's when we officially started our business, when we started doing the internet video thing full-time."[82]

They started by creating all sorts of videos, including music videos and sketches, and realized they were spending so much time together talking as friends they could easily turn that into a show.

Good Mythical Morning started as a ten-minute conversation about anything in Rhett's garage. It has obviously grown since then, but it's interesting to note that, over the years, while they developed *Good Mythical Morning*, other talk shows on mainstream television were trying to develop segments that would do well online with a viral quality, such as James Corden's *Carpool Karaoke*.

---

82 Abbey, Alison. "The Best Parts of Rhett & Link, Plus an Exclusive Interview With the Internet's Kings of Comedy." *Parade.* May 19, 2017.

But Rhett & Link were there first, and they are still doing it quite well.

* * *

While it may seem like a dream to work and laugh with your best friend all the time, if you think about it for a few minutes, you might be a little apprehensive.

How do you *work* with your best friend? How do you keep coming up with new things consistent with your brand? And what happens when you run out of ideas?

Luckily, Rhett & Link have thought this through during their years of experience.

First, on working with your best friend, they view each other as both friends and business partners.

Rhett says, "We're pretty practical. We both have engineering degrees. Even when we started this ten years ago, it was very small. No one was taking it seriously, no one knew where the platform was going to go, but we still came into an office from 9 to 6 every single day. We treated it like a business."[83]

---

83 Ibid

That right there is a good first step, but I will also add the importance of not just communication but also transparency. If this is a serious endeavor intended to make money for both of you, both should have a say in decisions. You should be open and honest, or it just won't work out.

Perhaps having a daily or weekly session to brainstorm ideas and talk through the general state of the business details will guarantee that both thoughts and concerns will be heard. Especially at the beginning of your partnership, making sure you are both on the same page in terms of goals is vital to your shared success. Knowing what each person can bring to the table in terms of knowledge and skills for any aspect of the business and creative process can make things smoother.

Also, having an impartial third person to call in for any disagreements might not be a bad idea either.

Rhett continues, "I don't think we fight any more than we did then. We don't take it any more seriously than we did back then, which was very seriously. We always have fun, though, and we always make each other laugh; that's kind of the litmus test for when we know we've got a good idea, when we both laugh at it. That aspect of the job is still there."[84]

Ah, yes. The fun. If you get *too* bogged down in the work, you can lose the fun and your content will suffer for it. Remember, the goal is to be creatively fulfilled.

About creating new content consistent with their brand, they make each other laugh with some of the ridiculous things they come up with for *Good Mythical Morning*, especially involving food.

Rhett says, "The structure of that show is such that we put ourselves in situations where just being ourselves is where the humor comes from."[85]

As long as they keep making each other laugh, they won't run out of ideas. They are lucky enough that their humor is accessible for not just a wide demographic of viewers, but also in terms of being monetizable on YouTube.

Link says, "Rated E for everyone...It's not risky for brands, and it's accessible to families. Our core demo

84 Abbey, Alison. "The Best Parts of Rhett & Link, Plus an Exclusive Interview With the Internet's Kings of Comedy." *Parade.* May 19, 2017.
85 Ibid

is college-aged, but we have fans come up to us on the street, and it would be like a mom or a dad and a high schooler or middle schooler. It's hard for us to tell who's the bigger fan, the parent or the kid. That turns out to be great for business, but that was just a byproduct of our comedic instincts. And also, in terms of marketers' interests and YouTube, we've been able to bypass any perceived controversy that's out there, because of the nature of our content."[86]

That is another way they have been very successful— YouTube likes them, a wide demographic of people like them. It's basic marketing. They have their audience.

Creator-to-Creator Tip #14
Treat your project as seriously as you want to— but always remember to keep fun at the core!

Speaking of audience, as with any other online creator, their audience plays a key part in maintaining the content they want to create. It isn't just the two of them having fun in a vacuum.

Link says, "We listen to our artistic voice, we listen to each other, and we listen to our audience. It's a discipline to comb through comments and find the collective wis-

---

86 Ibid

dom of people who are impulsive, passive, sometimes negative, but there's something there that you can always glean that can inform the next thing you do."[87]

And, really, it is the audience that decides if you are going to "get big" or not. They are the ones that view, that share, that comment. So, for Rhett & Link, the audience has always been an integral part of their growing process.

Link says, "We've been on YouTube since the beginning of YouTube, because there was no barrier for us to create our own channel and to just put our content out there. It was up to the viewers to decide whether they actually wanted to view it or not. It's always been a very direct relationship with us...We experimented with a lot of things. We had success with a lot of different things over the more than a decade, and some failures that we all forget about until someone sees them."[88]

Don't forget—the audience is not just a passive group of people. They care about you and your content, and

87 Ifeanyi, KC. "Inside The "Mythical" Minds And Digital Empire Of You-Tube Pioneers Rhett & Link." *Fast Company*. March 29, 2017.

88 Abbey, Alison. "The Best Parts of Rhett & Link, Plus an Exclusive Interview With the Internet's Kings of Comedy." *Parade*. May 19, 2017.

you can have a special relationship when the audience becomes a core part of your development as a creator.

Here's my main takeaway from their story: you won't succeed right away. Your million-dollar idea might not be the first thing you create, and it certainly won't be perfect right away.

But it's okay to try and fail. Listen to your audience. And absolutely don't be discouraged if you don't take off right away.

There are some special circumstances and magical (dare I say mythical) moments that align and create something wonderful, such as the on-camera friendship, humor, and chemistry found with Rhett & Link, that cannot be replicated. Not all of us have best friends who have been with us for decades, and not everyone has perfectly advertiser-friendly humor.

Part of my current interest in making videos stems from projects some very creative friends and I made while we were in elementary and middle school. I was usually the person behind the camera and editing, and they would improv a loose story or skit, often set to music. These projects will never be shown to a public audience, but to pique your interest, they included wrestling with a giant stuffed bear, aliens carrying around bread, and Squirmles dancing to "Istanbul not Constantinople."

For a class project (starring maybe ten classmates for computer class), we did a parody of *Leave it to Beaver* called *Leave it to Bieber.* Make of that what you will.

Just from my own experience, I find it entirely plausible that long-time creative friends who know each other's personalities and humor so well can make an entertainment YouTube channel into their living. Honestly, if we were a bit older and knew how the internet worked beyond how to look up *Harry Potter Puppet Pals* videos and play Club Penguin, this could have been us.

* * *

While it doesn't work for everyone, having a friend along the journey with you might be a big help. Many YouTubers in this book are solo acts and have noted they have benefitted when there was someone to help out, even just a little with editing or production. Imagine sharing the "talent" portion of the channel. It might seem less daunting to just get started.

Perhaps you have a friend who has a similar sense of humor or complements your personality. It might take a few tries to get used to each other and find the best content for your personalities. Be honest and open about your thoughts and goals for the project from the beginning. Make sure you are both on the same page, especially when making big business decisions. Keep your workplace fun with brainstorming sessions for content ideas and scheduling time just to talk, improvise, and laugh together.

Sometimes, if things are not working out, the smartest thing to do is to dissolve the partnership. Having a plan in place beforehand about what happens to the channel and the content in the event of a dissolution can help ensure a clean break.

You don't have to start with a partner right away. So many options are available, and it might take some time to find the thing that clicks just right.

Link says, "There's a constant threat of creating something that expresses what we think is funny and building on something that is working; when you do a daily show like *Good Mythical Morning*, it's easy to get in a rut and just do the things that are going to perform."[89]

---

89 Ifeanyi, KC. "Inside The "Mythical" Minds And Digital Empire Of You-Tube Pioneers Rhett & Link." *Fast Company*. March 29, 2017.

But they combat that. Rhett says, "We try to maintain the spirit of innovation and originality that characterized our content from the early days and translate that into every project that we're doing so it doesn't ever feel like it's coming from a corporate place."[90]

In other words, just have fun!

---

90 Ibid

Chapter 7

The Remix Technique

How do I come up with a channel topic?

How do you become a successful YouTuber? What if the answer was as simple as "do your research"?

It's not a bad idea, especially if you don't know exactly what you want the subject or format of your channel or other creative endeavor to be. Research is a good place to start. There are a few ways to go about doing this, but one such idea was described to me by the creator of the channel Because Geek, Val Carias.

She thinks the key to becoming a successful YouTuber is to first decide you want to be a YouTuber and recognize all the hard work that will go into it. Then, just apply what she calls the remix technique.

So what is the remix technique?

She says, "Pick something that you know is already working."[91] By this, she means a video style or channel subject that consistently gets views. You'll probably find something like this in more specific topics you are interested in (like certain television shows, books, movies, celebrities, and hobbies).

Val continues, "Find something that's already proving to be working, not something that a ton of people are doing because it might be too saturated. But if it's something that only a few people are doing, that's pretty good. So you pick that one thing, as long as you yourself like it, of course, and then add your own twist to it."[92]

Basically, if you watch videos where a lot of people use their phones to make videos of their dogs doing tricks in their backyards with some encouraging off-camera comments and perhaps a royalty-free cheerful song added to the background, which get a few hundred thousand views, you could make your own following that same formula.

Or you could record your dog doing tricks, perhaps with commentary added later of not just your thoughts but

---

91 Carias, Val in discussion with the author, January 24, 2019.
92 Ibid

your dog's thoughts, or more epic or rock music in the background because this was a hard trick.

Why is this her main tip for how to succeed on YouTube? This is essentially how she created her channel, Because Geek.

She says, "I started by watching a lot of YouTube...and then I started realizing that people were making money from it."[93] She had many ideas for content that were not monetizable because they would fall outside of Fair Use (for that definition, see Chapter 1). Then she landed on the idea of making *Game of Thrones* lore videos because she was a fan of medieval fantasy in general.

While she did start with a lore video (about the ancient history of the world of *Game of Thrones*), Because Geek did not take off until Val made a video talking about something no one else had yet—speculation and information based on the actual filming of the show, or "filming news."

She says, "It did feel like I was the first to make a sleuthing video on a filming news leaked picture from the sets of the filming...it was just the perfect timing, because it

---

93 Carias, Val in discussion with the author, January 24, 2019.

was when the *Game of Thrones* show was in the middle of a huge cliffhanger...it was just the biggest cliffhanger ever in history and everyone was talking about it. And so everyone went to YouTube to look for YouTube videos about what people were saying about it."[94]

Val's video was about a picture taken of Kit Harington on set and her reasons why the picture was not of the filming of a flashback but of an alive Jon Snow.[95]

She continues, "That video got so many views that I just started making more of that and eventually my channel just blew up. In about a year, I had reached 50,000 subscribers just from making the *Game of Thrones* filming news videos."[96]

While that video is not her most-watched video (that honor goes to a season 6 prediction/theory video in which she collaborated with a popular *Game of Thrones* fan artist[97]), it does have over 100,000 views, and for being one of her first ten videos, that is very good.

---

94 Ibid

95 Because Geek. "FULL ANALYSIS of leaked Kit Harington on set picture - Game of Thrones S06 News." YouTube video, 7:26. Posted [September 2015].

96 Carias, Val in discussion with the author, January 24, 2019.

97 Because Geek. "Game of Thrones Season 6 - The Proud Lord's Dead - Stark Revenge." YouTube video, 25:44. Posted [April 2016].

This is how the remix technique worked for her: there were other *Game of Thrones* channels out there, but as far as she could tell, she was the only one making hypotheses based on leaked set photos.

Other channels might have been creating lore videos or giving their reviews or reactions of episodes, but the "sleuthing" videos are the Because Geek twist. And she has enjoyed a successful channel because of it. She still makes reviews and lore videos, but the sleuthing videos with the spyglass icon on the thumbnail are Val's signature.

Creator Need-to-Know Definition:
Thumbnail—The unmoving preview image of video content. Paired with a title, the thumbnail is one way to entice viewers to watch the video.

The remix strategy would work well for creating channels about media-centered fandoms and other related secondary content. For something as big as *Game of Thrones*, a whole subcommunity of channels is centered around the same content.

According to the remix technique, each of them should have a twist to make them unique. Many of Val's friends are *Game of Thrones* YouTubers, who all started at about the same time, in the summer of 2015 (one of these is Chris from Smokescreen, from Chapter 4).

She says, "We were helping each other out, how to make better videos and all that. And you start talking and eventually you become friends."[98] She likes becoming friends with people before she collaborates. Once there is a friendship in place, the collaborations are successful.

Creator-to-Creator Tip #15

Since YouTube is a visual medium, keep in mind the importance of not just the content of the videos, but the thumbnails themselves. A personal brand encompasses not just the content and format of the videos; it could also include the thumbnails and titles. You could have a little symbol, like Val's spyglass, or a certain way of wording your titles. If we go back to Sean Evans and *Hot Ones* for a minute, those titles include the interviewee name and a present-tense action relating to the episode, such as "Key & Peele Lose Their Minds Eating Spicy Wings."[99]

Don't underestimate thumbnails, either, in driving traffic to your video (I'll get to this in a few paragraphs). Videos might include clickbait phrases or pictures in the thumbnails, while the titles might seem neutral. I see many theory videos use arrows and circles to give a quick preview of the content—and it has worked on me and thousands of others. Yes, creating thumbnails might include learning some new skills, or you can farm it out to a freelance graphic designer. Just something to think about.

---

98 Carias, Val in discussion with the author, January 24, 2019.

99 First We Feast. "Key & Peele Lose Their Minds Eating Spicy Wings | Hot Ones." YouTube video, 14:10. Posted [April 2016].

Story time.

I have, in fact, used the remix technique before, without realizing I was using it. I was inspired by the content of many YouTubers like Val and Chris leading up to and during Season 7 of *Game of Thrones*. That was right after I finished uploading to my channel the videos from that first personal project where I explored different video types.

I decided to create videos after each episode aired like every other *Game of Thrones*, film critic, and entertainment channels would do after the episodes, because why not?

I called my video series "RE3," which I thought was a pretty clever way of saying REcap, REact, REview. I would go through the episode scene by scene, summarizing it in my own words (recap). I would share my feelings or thoughts (react). And then I would give more critical opinions and give little theories for the next episode (review).

My way of remixing the traditional formula is by making my videos a whole mix of the kinds of videos that would normally come out by more established channels. They weren't just reaction videos, and I wasn't explaining hidden callbacks to less careful viewers. I was literally just saying the thoughts I had as I watched.

Really. I watched it when it aired for an initial viewing, and then I watched it again the next day with a Word doc open on the other half of the screen that pretty much became my script.

Did these videos blow up?

Absolutely not.

My most views were from the 4th episode, on which the thumbnail is me with a very shocked face, instead of a smile or neutral face like the other videos. That was some interesting data and lends credence to the idea that thumbnail has a lot to do with driving traffic to a video.

But what did I get out of it? I got to practice writing, being on camera, and making thumbnails with transparent images of characters from the episode (using my extremely limited Photoshop program and skills, which made me feel the most like a "real" YouTuber).

I took what I learned from watching and observing hundreds of other videos, and I then did my own thing. You can too!

Many of the videos for that aforementioned personal project could possibly be described as "remixed" as well. For example, instead of just making an edit of all my favorite *How I Met Your Mother* catchphrases with clips from the show and call it "Ten Best Catchphrases from *HIMYM*," I put on a suit jacket and did my best impersonations (as one of the leads always wears a suit and loves to say "suit up!" to those not wearing one).

Creator-to-Creator Tip #16
Several videos for my project were simply list videos—that example is from my five reasons why I love *How I Met Your Mother* video, which is a popular video format in the same way listicles are a popular blog format. It's a simple way to organize many thoughts, and if the video is "counting down" to the number one whatever, that is another great way to keep audience eyes on the video until the very end.

Creator-to-Creator Tip #17
Do your research!

Creator-to-Creator Tip #18
Val says, "Make sure of what you're getting into. Make sure it's what you want to do, because it's a very tough job, 24/7...And it can get difficult at times...it can get lonely. So again, have friends who are doing the same with you...Always try to remember what kind of person you are and try

to tailor your channel to that type of person...
And then always ask yourself what do you want
your audience to feel? That's a good question to
answer before you make a video."[100]

———————————————————————

* * *

So is becoming a successful YouTuber as easy as doing some research?

Definitely not, but research is a good place to start. This is true for not just what your channel will be about, but for all the behind-the-scenes work as well before you get started.

Sometimes things are out of your control. For example, timing can have a lot to do with whether a channel becomes popular. That is the case with Val's Because Geek, but it won't happen to everyone.

But paying attention to timing and looking for an optimal time to upload a video is another kind of research you can do, just in case. This depends on the kind of content you are producing, of course, but things like entertainment, sports, music, and technology have release dates, anniversaries, and special events you can keep in mind when releasing your content.

———————————

100 Carias, Val in discussion with the author, January 24, 2019.

Do you want to be a YouTuber but don't know where to begin? Try the remix technique!

First, you need to come up with a few ideas. Try things you like or things you enjoy watching. The more ideas the better, and maybe you can combine the ideas. Then, watch other channels with that content. Make notes of what you like and don't like. Think about ways you can change it. Apply the remix technique. Figure out how much work would go into that kind of content, what skills you already have, and where you might need to hire someone or learn a new skill.

No matter what, just go for it!

Chapter 8

Committing to a Hobby

What if I want to try something new?

Maybe you don't want to do something that's already been done. Maybe you want to do something completely new and see if it takes off. It is possible, even today, when it seems like someone has already thought of everything.

Here is one way to do it. All you need is a hobby.

Seeing "a gap in the market," knowing how to fill it, and being willing to commit to something are good ways to kick off a YouTube career.

Andrew Rea is the creator of the channel Binging with Babish where, among other things, he recreates famous dishes as seen in movies and television shows. Starting in 2016 when he recreated the beef vs. turkey burger cookoff from *Parks and Recreation*, Andrew has developed a comfortable following, as people want to see what he will come up with next.

His channel has grown exponentially over the past couple of years. In July 2017, he hit one million subscribers.[101] At the time of this writing, he has over five million. That's...a lot.

Pop Culture Plug
Parks and Recreation is an NBC sitcom with seven seasons airing between 2009 and 2015 about the wacky requests coming through the Pawnee, Indiana parks and recreation department and the lives of the colorful cast of characters who work there. It is the source of such pop culture ideas as "Treat Yo Self" and "Galentine's Day." The aforementioned beef vs. turkey burger cookoff was featured in episode 3x10 called "Soulmates."

But Andrew didn't start YouTube to gain this massive following. In fact, at first he didn't identify as much of a cook at all.

He says, "I'm a filmmaker, not a cook. And I had watched a lot of food videos on YouTube and I saw a gap in the market, where food content was not food-oriented

101 Binging with Babish. "Binging with Babish 1 Million Subscriber Special: Taco Town & Behind the Scenes." YouTube video, 8:38. Posted [July 2017].

enough, in my mind. So I decided that I would make this show specifically about the food. I am literally a backdrop to the food. That's why I wear a black apron, so the food pops more."[102]

It took him a while to reveal his face at all, though he has shown it more as he has become a more recognizable personality. The food itself is more important to him.

Interestingly, he calls himself a "student of YouTube cookery. [YouTube] changed the way I cook. I didn't go to culinary school. If I want to learn how to make something, I'm going to YouTube."[103]

And that's a great thing about YouTube in general—it can be a place for people to learn something new or something they might not have picked up originally. He says, "It's an exciting time to be a home cook, thanks to YouTube."[104]

There is an instantaneous way to gain information or view videos to walk you through a process, whether it

---

102 Margine, Claire. "The Creator Behind "Binging with Babish" Goes to Sleep Watching YouTube." *The Kitchn.* July 26, 2018.

103 Ibid

104 Ibid

is cooking, cars, or crafts. It's part of the magic of the internet, not just YouTube.

You can be well-known for having a cooking channel on YouTube whether you went to culinary school or not. Like with so many creators, it all depends on whether you want to put in the work to learn something new—and whether you will be creatively or otherwise fulfilled when you are done.

Andrew had his own motivation as well: "I got a chef's knife and whisk tattoo on my forearm about five years ago, before I was a halfway decent cook, as a way to 'hold myself hostage' into becoming a better one."[105]

Hey, whatever works for you.

* * *

The channel started almost by accident after he was experimenting with food photography for some free-lance work. He says, "I realized I had a good setup for a show and decided to make one episode for fun. People responded positively, I kept making it, and it kept

105 Maher, Michael. "Interview: Behind the Scenes with YouTube's Binging with Babish." *Premium Beat.* July 18, 2017.

growing—now I'm lucky enough to have made it my full-time job!"[106]

Andrew still does most of the work independently. "It's something that I originally was doing after work when my friends would be asleep and I needed a hobby."[107]

He does have other small series on his channel, including *Basics with Babish* where he shows viewers how to make more basic and everyday foods like brownies and eggs, which can sometimes require more of a film crew. But, he says, "it's mostly just me... I shoot in my kitchen, in my apartment, and then I bring it over to the living room where I edit it. Then I'm usually posting it the next day."[108]

Even though he does most of the work himself, he wouldn't have gotten this far without his supportive audience, especially when it comes to getting ideas for what kind of dish he should make next.

He says, "For the most part, I go to my audience for inspiration. I'm constantly getting comments about

106 Ibid

107 "Binging with Babish's Andrew Rea on the Secret to his Success." *Milk Street.* November 20, 2018.

108 Ibid

what viewers want to see recreated on my show. I've put a huge effort into constantly and reliably interacting with my audience, and I think it's been helpful in the growth of my channel, both in building a fanbase and finding new ideas I hadn't considered!"[109]

This reiterates yet again the importance of not just interacting with an audience but listening to an audience. The audience can have a direct impact on the channel and have even more of a connection and loyalty to the creator. Something they come up with is on the channel. They participated, however directly or indirectly, in the direction of their entertainment.

How cool is that?

Andrew feels a strong connection to his audience. Most of them are between eighteen and thirty-five.

He says, "They're right in the sweet spot when people are just getting out of college, or they're young adults who are learning to live on their own and picking up new hobbies. It reminds me very much of myself five

109 Maher, Michael. "Interview: Behind the Scenes with YouTube's Binging with Babish." *Premium Beat.* July 18, 2017.

years ago. It's people who are learning how to cook away from home."[110]

People are looking for a way to connect and interact with their content. They don't want to just be entertained—they want to be informed. Andrew sees that is the direction YouTube, and especially the food-on-YouTube sub-genre, is going. It is moving away from following trends and trying to be the next, flashiest, viral thing.

He says, "People are interested in content that entertains them, that keeps them engaged, but also is as informative as it is fun."[111] People can choose from a lot of content when they go onto the internet, so you want to make their time, subscription, and possible comment, worth their while.

Andrew has responded accordingly to this trend. He takes the time to put more effort into some of his videos, such as recreating a wok over a fire from the video game *Zelda: Breath of the Wild.*

---

110 Margine, Claire. "The Creator Behind "Binging with Babish" Goes to Sleep Watching YouTube." *The Kitchn.* July 26, 2018.

111 Margine, Claire. "The Creator Behind "Binging with Babish" Goes to Sleep Watching YouTube." *The Kitchn.* July 26, 2018.

He says, "The more seriously I take it, the more people seem to like that...I could have made something that tastes exactly the same in a wok at home, but people definitely like how far I take it."[112]

The audience is entertained as well as informed and can definitely appreciate the effort that went into the creation.

Being successful online comes down portraying your passion. He says, "People need to like you and feel how passionate you are about something. Find something you love so much you have to yell at other people about it. Just find something that drives you crazy and share it with the world."[113]

Creator-to-Creator Tip #19
Find something you are passionate about and share it!

I can definitely relate to that feeling! While I do not upload regularly or have a "normal" format for my content, the videos I create often stem from what I am obsessed with at the moment. I feel like the only way I can communicate my delight and obsession is by making

---

112 "Binging with Babish's Andrew Rea on the Secret to his Success." *Milk Street.* November 20, 2018.

113 Ibid

a video and hoping other people who enjoy the subject find it.

My favorite of these is when I reviewed *Mozart in the Jungle*, an Amazon show about the New York Symphony and an oboist. As I am an oboist, I thought it would be fun to not just talk about an actress's portrayal of my instrument alongside my other observations as a critical viewer and storyteller, but also to play a little music.

When I talked about the oboe pieces I recognized and favorite pieces I would like to hear in the next season, I literally played them. (The video was created before the news broke the show was canceled.) I even quickly taught myself the first phrase of the signature piece of the show, the third movement of Mozart's *Concerto for Oboe in C*, which I hadn't learned before.

There have been a few nice comments on the video, talking about how they loved the show too. One in particular mentioned they were inspired to go to orchestral concerts and eventually bought season tickets because of the show!

It is also my second-most-viewed video, with over two thousand views as I am writing. The title and thumbnail might have a bit to do with it (*"Mozart in the Jungle*

Seasons 1–4 Review—by an oboist!" with my oboe on full display), but I also hope my recitation of the script exudes the passion I will always feel for music.

In this video, I used my hobby (can you call it a hobby if you have a music degree?) and my passion for that hobby to communicate the message.

Who knows? I might be making more oboe videos in the future. It seems like most YouTube musicians are pianists, vocalists, or violinists. By comparison, there are not many videos of oboes. There might be a gap I can fill.

* * *

So maybe you can't cook. That's okay. Is there some kind of video you've always wanted to see? Something you're curious about? Maybe you have a hobby you want to invest a little more time into. Try something new, commit to your hobby, and share it with the world.

Chapter 9

A Fusion of Interests

What if I like/am good at a few different things?

Admit it, you've used Google Translate at some point—probably to squeak through some high school assignment at the last minute (me), or maybe you were curious about something you heard in a movie. Google Translate is a powerful tool, but it's not perfect, especially when a phrase is run through a series of languages and then back into English. The results can be...unintelligible.

But Malinda Kathleen Reese, creator of the popular *Google Translate Sings* music video series on YouTube, did just that.

It started as procrastination (see, procrastination can be good!) and a little too much listening to "Let It Go" (remember when that was popular?). She was listening to the Disney version, where twenty-five women from different countries sang the song in their language.

When she recognized one line did not translate directly back into English, she wondered what the rest of the video directly translated to.

She ran the lyrics through different languages in Google Translate several times to create multiple layers of translation, building one on top of the other.

She says, "And finally, after the fourth layer, it came up with 'give up' (which is the translation of "let it go") and I thought, *'Oh dear God, this is awful and funny, and wow, this is too good for me not to share.'* In about two hours, I made the whole video and put it up on private for friends and family to see. My friends were like "'you need to make this public'," and I did, and things went from there."[114]

And this is what she's done ever since.

She takes pop songs and musical songs and runs them through Google Translate. Over the years there has been a gradual rise in production quality from the "Let It Go" video (which looks like a practice room, a standard podcast mic, and a basic camera) to better cameras and recording equipment, sets and props, and elaborate

114 "Malinda Kathleen Reese Extended Interview." *Mixcloud*. Podcast, 25:01. Posted [November 2015].

costumes to complete the overall aesthetic or character she is going for in the video.

These costumes evoke the character or artist whose song she is portraying, recreating iconic looks such as Miley Cyrus's white background and red lips from "Wrecking Ball" ("I came in like a wrecking ball" turned into "I like the ball in the sink"[115]) or the unsubtle theatricality of King George from *Hamilton* (when the popular character song "You'll Be Back" becomes "That Behind"[116]).

Malinda also provides the original lyrics on-screen as well for reference so viewers can see just how out of whack the result is. All this goes together to provide the audience with a music video, complete with lyrics they're probably not expecting.

Creator-to-Creator Tip #20
It took two hours to make the "Let it Go" video. The original video provides a brief explanation and features her singing the newly translated lyrics next to a muted clip of the song from *Frozen*.[117] The new lyrics on the bottom of the video are playing subtitle-style as she sings

---

115 Translator Fails. "Google Translate Sings: "Wrecking Ball" by Miley Cyrus (PARODY)." YouTube video, 4:56. Posted [June 2014].

116 Translator Fails. "Google Translate Sings: You'll Be Back from Hamilton." YouTube video, 5:02. Posted [September 2016].

117 Translator Fails. ""Let It Go" from Frozen according to Google Translate (PARODY)." YouTube video, 4:29. Posted [February 2014].

them. With minimal cuts in the video itself, the editing portion would have taken the longest, especially creating the subtitles. Based on experience, I think two hours to make that four-and-a-half-minute video is plausible.

Editing can be the longest part of the video creation process, even if you have a strategy to get through the raw footage like I do. If I have an hour of raw footage, I'm looking at around three+ hours of editing. Adding extras like subtitles, overlays, pictures, and music can take even longer. What I'm trying to say here is...plan ahead. If you think it takes a long time to film something, try editing!

On YouTube, she balances two channels. The first is dedicated to the *Translator Fails* that launched her to fame in the first place (though it includes both serious covers with actual lyrics like Kesha's "Praying" or "Never Enough" from *The Greatest Showman*, as well as *Google Translate Fails* of everyday things like airplane safety instructions or makeup tutorials).

On the second channel, she puts out original songs, vlogs talking about what's on her mind or other random things like answering fan questions (by singing her answers). This second channel is more of a personal outlet and it's aptly called MALINDA.

Becoming a YouTuber was not what Malinda planned on doing with her life, but she has whole-heartedly embraced this unexpected path that combines several of her interests and strengths.

She went to school for acting, which is what she would be doing full-time "had YouTube not wandered into my life. At this point, I'm pursuing YouTube as a career because that's what I'm finding I'm most passionate about, and Patreon is the reason I'm able to do that, honestly. And acting has always been something I've done as a passion."[118]

But it's not just acting that makes her channels a success. Because her main output is the *Google Translate Sings* videos, she also had to be strong with music and comedy to sell the paradoxical serious and goofy parodies.

Music was always a passion for her, but the comedy was a bit more unexpected.

"To be honest, I never thought I'd do comedy. I grew up as an actor and a musician, and I always loved doing comedy as an actor. But the sort of comedy that comes from "you," created comedy that's personal and more like sketches and that sort of thing. Never thought I'd do that."[119]

---

118 "Malinda Kathleen Reese Extended Interview." *Mixcloud*. Podcast, 25:01. Posted [November 2015].

119 Ibid

She is using her drama school skills and onstage experiences on top of learning how to use technology to create comedy.

And this is why she loves doing what she does on YouTube.

"YouTube is very much a fusion of everything I grew up doing. And I was never a person to settle on one thing; I always had to do a million things at once. And so it's a great fusion where I can do everything at once and that's part of the job, which is exciting for me."[120]

Being a YouTuber requires you to wear many hats and perhaps learn new technological and/or business skills, but if you can take things you are already good at and turn them into a compelling channel, do that!

Creator-to-Creator Tip #21
Some YouTubers have a second channel where they might put more personal or behind-the-scenes content. In some cases, it seems like a leftover from the days before Patreon when you wanted your primary channel to be clean with just your final product and only your most dedicated fans would bother subscribing to your second channel. I've noticed more and more "second channels" I subscribed to have been used less and less lately. It could also be a

---

120 Ibid

> personal or branding choice, where you want to
> make content that you feel does not belong on
> your main channel. Starting out, you probably
> don't need a second channel.

She is very humble about her successes and shares how she deals with adjusting to having a prominent online presence.

Malinda says, "[Going viral] emphasizes the difference between my online life and my real-time life. Suddenly, my focus in my real-time life must become a lot more intense, and I have to make sure I'm still fulfilling my commitments with my friends. It's humbling because the rest of your life doesn't change. You still have to go to rehearsal with your friends and write an essay if you're in college."[121]

This, if anything, should emphasize how much those people who go viral are ordinary people, just like you. Even if they are famous for their fifteen minutes, or build a channel that consistently goes viral, they still have everyday responsibilities to maintain.

She continues, "It's a humbling, grounding experience any time a video goes viral. That's one thing I look for-

---

121 Drew's Corner—Drew C. Ryan. "MALINDA KATHLEEN REESE (GOO-GLE TRANSLATE SINGS) INTERVIEW—Reel Geek Girls #70." YouTube video, 9:24. Posted [November 2017].

ward to—being reminded of the difference between the two and enjoying how I can have those two things be separate."[122]

That is something to keep in mind—going viral doesn't have to change your everyday life. You are still the same person to the people closest to you, and you should not ignore them.

If compartmentalizing works, try doing that. Make time to hang out with people, or even better, schedule time—lunch with your mom every Tuesday or something like that. Leave your video ideas, filming, editing, and business details in your office or at your home when you leave it.

You could also force yourself to only work on projects for so many hours in a day or a week.

Creator-to-Creator Tip #22
Take breaks from social media on occasion! It does everyone a world of good to get away, but even more so when you have constant interactions with an audience. Tell your followers you will be taking a break, then do. If you want a clean break, go for a month. But I have also seen people take the weekends to reconnect with the "real-time world."

---

122 Ibid

And speaking of advice, her advice about starting on YouTube is to just do it!

She says, "Your own inability to just press that upload button is the only thing that's gonna hold you back. So press the upload button. Just do it. Definitely start with things that you make from the heart and send them out there, quickly."[123]

I absolutely agree with that. There is no way you can practice a certain skill, or improve on your concept, or any of the other advice from this book if you don't put something out there in the first place! No one can comment on or share your video if you don't have a video.

It can be daunting to press the "publish" button and put yourself out there. I get it—but it's part of being a creator. You must be willing to put a piece of yourself out there in the open and be vulnerable to whatever comes your way.

Malinda echoes others in this book when she goes into the heart of what she thinks is so great about YouTube.

---

123 "Malinda Kathleen Reese Extended Interview." *Mixcloud.* Podcast, 25:01. Posted [November 2015].

She says, "I think what's so unique about YouTube is because there is that value of authenticity, and if you are fake in any way, they can smell it and tell you. As a result, the people that are successful are the people that are doing what they love because they are passionate about it. And it just sets a great example. If you're passionate about it, that's what people are going to respond to. As long as it's real and comes from your heart, then people do respond."[124]

It's all about authenticity and doing what you love. Do what you want but do it with passion. People can tell when there is some spark of excitement behind the camera, in everything that you do. You must want to do this to be successful.

Creator-to-Creator Tip #23
Just do it! You can't get any feedback if you don't publish anything.

---

* * *

When coming up with a concept, consider fusion—a combination of interests, implementing different technologies and social media platforms, using a variety of tools, honing a variety of skills, and finding a balance

---

124 Ibid

between pleasing your audience and maintaining your passion.

Does anything come to mind? Take a minute to brainstorm and write down all your interests and hobbies. Try pairing up two that are very different and see if you can make them work together. Is there an intersection between these interests? Do some research—is anyone else combining these two things? Then consider how you could make money off what you are doing. Can you sell it as a product? Raise funds on a livestream? (For example, if you can play piano and like video games, you can play video game music live and take requests, as YouTube and Twitch streamer lara6683 has done.[125]) Is Patreon the only way to go? Then make a mental projection of what your endeavor could look like. Are you being authentic? Are you enjoying what you are doing?

In other words, are you fulfilled?

---

125 Lara6683. "Mega Medley that was supposed to be 5 minutes but wasn't." YouTube video, 1:25:12. Posted [November 2017].

Chapter 10

Hey Brother!

What if I have no idea of what to do?

I started this section by talking about one YouTube duo, Rhett & Link, so I thought I should end it with another YouTube duo. Maybe you don't have a best friend you can start a channel with. Perhaps there is someone a little closer to home...like your brother. Imagine if every day you could talk about your favorite fandoms with your brother! For J and Ben Carlin, their YouTube channel, Super Carlin Brothers, gives them the chance to make their living together while talking nerdy topics and fun fan theories.

Super Carlin Brothers started when, post-college, the two brothers were living in the same house. J had the idea for them to have a conversation through video, just like the Vlogbrothers from Chapter 1, Hank and John Green. They did five videos a week, trading who was in the video for a year, and for fun, they kept to themselves the fact they were living in the same house!

Ben says, "That was our big reveal at the end of Year One—that we had been sitting in the same room for the whole time. And that was the first time we got the taste of comment after comment of people saying, 'Whoa, mind blown!'"[126]

They would definitely get more comments like that once they got into the business of fandom theories.

Their early videos were not about anything in particular; drawing much inspiration from the Vlogbrothers format, it was just a conversation between brothers that some people on the internet just happened to watch and enjoy.

That all changed during their second year.

J says, "That was in the middle of Year Two, and a couple of things happened all at once. First, at the time, coming up with a new video topic every single week was the hardest part of running the channel, and even sometimes still is...we had watched *Brave* and *Up* back

---

126 Emily. "Catching up with the Super Carlin Brothers: YouTube, Theories, Fandom, and More!" *Nerds and Beyond.* April 17, 2018.

to back...and I was looking up the Easter eggs I could have looked for in the movies."[127]

Creator Need-to-Know Definition:
Easter egg – In film, television, and video games, a hidden message, image, etc. that may not have to do with the main story but is instead hidden for careful viewers to find. The examples of Easter eggs found in Pixar movies include the phrase "A113," the Pizza Planet truck from *Toy Story*, and the colorful Luxo ball, as well as references to other Pixar movies.

"Then I talked to Tyler (their other brother!) and he said, 'Well, have you heard of this Pixar Theory thing?'...I thought it was the coolest thing ever. And I immediately said, 'Well, I know what my video for Tuesday is!'" [128]

On July 23, 2013, J uploaded The Pixar Theory. In this video, he explains the theory created by Jon Negroni that states all the Pixar movies take place in the same universe on the same timeline. It currently has over ten million views and is their most-watched video.[129]

Amid their Vlogbrothers talk-about-anything videos, they also uploaded occasional videos about Pixar and

---

127 Ibid

128 Emily. "Catching up with the Super Carlin Brothers: YouTube, Theories, Fandom, and More!" *Nerds and Beyond.* April 17, 2018.

129 SuperCarlinBrothers. "The Pixar Theory." YouTube video, 12:08. Posted [July 2013].

Disney, with Ben doing a series called *Pixar Fast Facts* and J making a video about snubbed Disney princesses (because apparently being an official Disney princess has requirements beyond being a princess in a Disney movie).

J says, "We didn't set out to do fandom stuff at the beginning," and regarding The Pixar Theory and related videos, "That was sort of the turning point. From there, it just exploded."[130]

This resulted in a shifting of the kinds of videos they created, a shift that has characterized their channel ever since. Now, they make videos about Disney and Pixar movies, franchises like *Harry Potter*, *Star Wars*, and Marvel, and other fandoms as well. They are seen as experts in these entertainment "fields."

Ben says, "Now when we make a video weighing in on something like *Harry Potter*, we have enough of a reputation where we feel like there is some value to our weigh-in because we've been making videos for so long."[131]

---

130 Emily. "Catching up with the Super Carlin Brothers: YouTube, Theories, Fandom, and More!" *Nerds and Beyond.* April 17, 2018.

131 Ibid

I definitely agree with this. Several videos they made after the release of *The Crimes of Grindelwald* helped me come to terms with parts I was confused by. Their theories explained parts of the movie that turned into a litany of common complaints made by fans (like how McGonagall couldn't have been in the flashbacks when she hadn't been born yet according to dates found in the original *Harry Potter* series).

They certainly have a knack for knowing the source material and going above and beyond to do research into the scripts and other canon sources of information (like *Harry Potter's* Pottermore) and laying out their trail of success.

Because they have been doing this for so long and so well, they have a massive following of just over two million subscribers (at the time of this writing).

Ben says, "Now it's cool that whenever a trailer comes out, people will start messaging and tweeting us and saying, 'Oh my God, I can't wait to see what you guys think about the new *Solo* trailer or the new *Incredibles 2* trailer.'" [132]

---

132 Emily. "Catching up with the Super Carlin Brothers: YouTube, Theories, Fandom, and More!" *Nerds and Beyond*. April 17, 2018.

Members of a fandom will go to them first about news concerning that fandom, perhaps before looking at official accounts. They're no longer just fans; they're experts too.

The creators have also experienced the power of a fandom and a community, not just around the fandoms they talk about each week, but around themselves as well. Through their Patreon and Discord server, they have met so many people.

One of the most common perks many creators offer through Patreon is access to a Discord server. Through this private chat room, creators can have conversations with members of their audience. But the creators don't even need to be present for the audience to use them—members of the Super Carlin Brothers audience have become friends with each other just chatting through Discord! This is another way to build a community around your channel.

Creator Need-to-Know Definition:
Discord – Discord started as a service for gamers so they could text or voice chat on private servers. Discord can run on a browser, or through an app on a computer or phone, giving users many options to take part in conversations. When a creator makes a private server, they can choose to share the link with only certain audience members or all

of them. There can also be private channels within servers, creating even more exclusivity if desired.

Like a Facebook fan page or website, Discord can be a place for community members to interact with just each other. The creator can set up their own moderation tools, called Discord bots, if they do not have a human moderator and can let the chat just go.

Discord is particularly appealing to livestreamers because of the flexibility of what those in the chat can do, including create longer posts and share images and GIFs, which they cannot do in YouTube or Twitch chatting. But it also works for regular audience members who just want to talk about (and with!) their favorite creators, with people who enjoy their content just as much as they do![133]

Because of this following, they have expanded to a gaming channel where they play games like *PokemonX* and *Super Smash Bros.*

On a completely unrelated note, they also launched their own coffee company, called Carlin Brothers Coffee, in September 2018.[134]

They announced the company in the video called "THE BIG ANNOUNCEMENT!" and continue to promote it on

---

133 Melcon, Andrew. "Discord: Everything You Need to Know." *Tom's Guide.* March 11, 2018.

134 SuperCarlinBrothers. "THE BIG ANNOUNCEMENT!" YouTube video, 4:34. Posted [September 2018].

their regular videos. This is an example of something more and more creators are starting to do.

These creators branch out into side businesses and sell a few items they are sure their audience will enjoy, and that they themselves believe in. For example, Philip DeFranco, who uses YouTube to run a news network, has a haircare and candle venture called Beautiful Bastard (named after what he calls his audience).

I think this will continue. Creators should embrace the idea of diversifying income sources and remaining creatively stimulated. And when the creator decides a project must come to an end, such as if a television show they are reviewing on a podcast finishes or they are tired of vlogging their life every single day, they have this second business to fall back on. Some creators have been in this YouTube business for more than a decade; sometimes to avoid burnout, you have to change directions completely.

Now, this may not be something you need to worry about right now. If you want to create, then create! But if starting a coffee company sounds more exciting than a YouTube channel, you might want to pursue that instead.

While they have come a long way from recent college
graduates talking to each other from across a house to
businessmen making their living talking about their
fandoms, the core of their videos remains the same. It
is a conversation between brothers, with J uploading on
Tuesdays and Ben uploading on Thursdays, and sometimes they upload together when they review new movies or compete in challenging quizzes forcing them to
remember minute details of *Harry Potter* lore.

But they still start every video with a "hey brother!"

Maybe they didn't start out having a specific goal in
mind for their channel. But due to some lucky timing
with content and some smart decisions on their part, the

Super Carlin Brothers were able to shift their channel focus to something more sought after on YouTube and more fun for them.

J says, "It's super fun. When we started making videos, it was sort of a vague pipe dream. Even when I imagined it being successful enough to be a full-time job, it was a version where I was barely making enough money and living at home. I never imagined having an office, or having brand deals, or having an employee. It is surreal and the ultimate dream job."[135]

* * *

The takeaway here is simple—maybe you don't have a specific idea for your creative endeavor. Maybe you just like [blank] and that's fine! The more you create and listen to your audience, the more likely what you want to create will form right in front of you.

Having a partner to bounce ideas off of or share the weekly workload can increase your chances of finding your channel topic—with double the number of ideas, you're more likely to hit the jackpot! And like the Super Carlin Brothers, maybe try a sibling as a partner. Since

135 Emily. "Catching up with the Super Carlin Brothers: YouTube, Theories, Fandom, and More!" *Nerds and Beyond*. April 17, 2018.

you have known each other for a long time, you will be familiar with their humor and creative abilities. This could make your project very fun and make you feel like kids again! However, just like when working with friends, the same rules apply if the partnership does not work out—have a plan in place and have a neutral third party for disputes.

No matter what you end up doing, you just have to give it a shot.

Part III

Life as Creator

You should have learned through these last few chapters there is more than one way to start a channel. It could stem from natural chemistry with a scene partner, remixing a popular idea, challenging yourself with a hobby, mixing a few things you are good at, or letting the channel mold itself.

Now you have your channel concept (or are well on your way to finding it, with brainstorming notes aplenty!) and are ready to roll!

I can understand the thrill of being on the precipice of a brand-new project and wanting to dive in one hundred percent. I know I've been there many times.

But before you start purchasing web domains and creating social media on every single platform, take a look at a little more advice first.

This final section continues the tour through YouTubers.

You will continue to explore different channel concepts and advice on how you can run your channel as a self-owned and self-motivated business.

You will also be introduced to ideas to keep in mind while running an active channel as a member of the YouTube community. Some of these include types of content you can create as well as other things you should remember when creating content and interacting with an audience.

Of course, at the center of it all is being creatively fulfilled.

You might be surprised at how some of the longest-creating and popular YouTubers still find ways to be creatively fulfilled each time they upload.

Pay attention and stay excited—you're almost ready to begin!

Chapter 11

Self-Motivation

What is it like to be a small, full-time YouTuber?

Ian Martin is not that different from other YouTubers in that he is full-time. Making episode-by-episode guides for Whedonverse television shows and in-depth philosophical movie reviews has drawn in a small but loyal fanbase for the channel Passion of the Nerd.

And here's the difference between him and many other full-time YouTubers—as of this writing, he is just shy of 35,000 subscribers, which is pennies compared to some others in this book.

That doesn't matter though.

What matters is that as a recent full-timer, Ian is making the transition from the channel being an exciting addition to his life as an escape from his full-time job to it being his full-time job.

That is quite a mindset shift. It's not technically hard since he's been making videos for so long, but it is difficult in its own way.

As he says, "It's rough. It's not rough in the sense of difficult, or rather, painful or any of that...It requires an entirely new set of muscles I've never had to exercise before. So going to an office and having a boss and having objectives in the company, things to do and people watching and people waiting for your work and so forth means that you don't have to develop a strong sense of self-discipline."[136]

Being told what to do is easier. Having goals already outlined for you and just playing your part is less stressful.

One way to combat this right away as a full-time YouTuber is to make your goals very clear, whatever it takes. It might be writing them down, printing them out and hanging them on your wall, or making sticky notes.

You could have different methods for short- and long-term goals. If you aren't sure how to get started, think back to a time when you had to set goals. For me, it's easiest to compare to planning when to do assignments

---

136 Martin, Ian in discussion with the author, January 29, 2019.

in college. You think week to week, month to month, building up to semester by semester.

So start small. Get the channel up and running, as well as social media. Set up Patreon, research sponsorships. Film and edit a few videos and have them in the can, ready to post ahead of time.

Then get a little larger. Once you are more used to creating content and know what you like doing, it might help to create a calendar of when videos will go up and put it somewhere visible in your workspace.

If you can see what your channel should look like this month, it might motivate you to actually get it there.

Then how do you reach the next goal, whether that is producing one video a week or even finishing the script you should have finished two days ago? There are a few ways.

Mainly, you need to keep yourself accountable. You can tell people close to you your next goal and then have them check on you close to your "deadline," almost like a boss or manager. If outside people are working with you on editing or graphics, have them check on you frequently.

You can post on your social media the date you will upload a video; your audience might keep you more accountable than friends or family would.

And of course, if this is your full-time job, you need to actually create something to be paid. Sometimes you just need a reminder of this to get to work.

Pop Culture Plug

"The Whedonverse" is the fandom term for the creations of Joss Whedon. These include the television shows *Buffy the Vampire Slayer, Angel, Firefly,* and *Dollhouse* (and sometimes Marvel's *Agents of S.H.I.E.L.D.*), the films *Cabin in the Woods* and *Much Ado About Nothing,* and the web miniseries musical *Dr. Horrible's Sing-Along Blog.* Many of these works can be considered cult classics, and attached to them all is a passionate group of fans. Some, like *Buffy/Angel* and *Firefly,* even have books and college courses about them, leading to a trend of closely studying these shows.

There's no hiding from the truth that when you're by yourself and you are motivating yourself, it can get tough.

When you're self-employed, as Ian says, "you have all the time in the world to hate what you're writing and to be sure that people are going to downvote the hell out of it and to hate what you did and to wonder if you're a fraud and this is pointless and I shouldn't be doing this or whatever it may be. Suddenly it's four days later and you haven't written anything. Not only that, you have to pull yourself out of that realm of self-doubt in order to actually start writing and get the next thing done or get the next thing filmed or what have you."[137]

Recognize that you are your own worst critic and then sit yourself down and start researching and writing a script—because you have an audience waiting and bills that need to be paid.

But it's not all bad! Everyone faces this and everyone gets through it. At the end of the day, you can be proud of what you have created. Everything you do is part of a learning process.

That is where Ian is right now: "in this very early stage of doing this, building those muscles...sort of getting up and being intentional and direct and sitting down and getting right to work and all of that because it is easy to not do that."[138]

You must retrain how you think about your work, how to approach something that was once just a hobby.

---

137 Martin, Ian in discussion with the author, January 29, 2019.
138 Martin, Ian in discussion with the author, January 29, 2019.

There's a certain danger in turning something you love into your living. If you try to force having fun or creativity when you aren't feeling it, you might start dreading what you once enjoyed doing, especially when it is tied to your living; the pressure is always on.

That is where being prepared and scheduled, having a plan, and having an audience support system will come in handy. If you need to take a break, take a break. If you can feel the work slipping past the normal stress and challenge of a creative project and into the territory of something you're just not looking forward to, it might be time to stop.

But if you do it right, you can enjoy it. Taking small breaks for inspiration, keeping to a schedule to avoid staying behind, and possibly hiring someone to help with part of the workload can relieve some of the stress and keep you from reaching the "dread" stage.

You can focus on the joy of creating. You can be fulfilled.

A lot of that can stem from having a loyal audience. Even if you are self-employed and do all your work yourself, as I mentioned before, your audience can hold you accountable.

They paid for Patreon for a reason—they like your content, so you should give them content. They take the time to interact with you and they care about you. So be honest with them. They'll be patient for the "good stuff" and will let you know if they don't like it.

Creator-To-Creator Tip #26
It will be HARD to transition to being a full-time creator, harder than you might think, especially in terms of motivation. Find ways to keep yourself accountable. From past school and work experience, you should know what works for you.

Speaking of Patreon and money, as a creator, you need to be smart. Depending on the content you create, YouTube revenue might not be enough to sustain a living. Even Patreon revenue might not be enough, especially if your channel is small and you do not have many audience members to begin with, let alone super loyal ones who would not mind tossing a dollar your way once a month.

Ian says, "I think any creator is smart to monetize as many different avenues as they have possible… For me, if Patreon shut down right now I'd be in trouble. So I think any creator is not just in the business of doing what they want to do, but selling themselves in as many ways as possible."[139]

Adding affiliate links and finding sponsorships might not be a bad idea in the grand scheme of things—while sponsors typically reach out to creators, you can join an affiliate program if you have a specific company or product in mind.

Like the Super Carlin Brothers and their coffee company, diversifying your income is not a bad idea. Audience members like merchandise as well! Just be smart and do your research ahead of time. If you feel taking on a particular sponsorship might compromise the inherent spirit of your content, don't do it. Try another one.

There are a few things at play here, and it is less about being a human making your living on the internet and more about being a self-motivated creative individual, which could apply to any freelance creator or self-employed individual.

I don't know much about that, but I do know about being in college and I think there's a bit of a correlation.

---

139 Martin, Ian in discussion with the author, January 29, 2019.

Yes, you want to get good grades and a degree and job by the end of it (comparable to getting, you know, *paid*).

But unlike with high school, where you can have your parents riding your back about getting assignments done, in college, it's all up to you. You don't want to disappoint your parents or professors, but in the end, it is on you to do the work.

And (surprise, surprise) I even felt some of that writing this book. Remind me not to take on another large assignment during my last semester of undergrad...or first semester of graduate school.

It's all about what you want to do and what you want to be. If you started a YouTube channel, there's a reason. If you started a podcast, a blog, or a book, there's a reason. You have something to say, you have a set of skills, and you have a potential audience to reach. You don't want to be stagnant.

Ian discovered something unique about YouTube when he finds a new creator. He says, "I love going to their videos and sorting by old and seeing their progression and their growth."[140]

---

140 Martin, Ian in discussion with the author, January 29, 2019.

That's his advice to new YouTubers. "You want to be the channel that people go to, search by old, and are like, wow, his old stuff was terrible because that means you're getting better, and moving in that direction is the most important aspect. You'll never be perfect, but you can always be getting better. And so that's sort of the sights that I set for my writing and my scripts and so forth, and that's where I suggest people do it first. Be a critical consumer of the things they love, and then apply that to their own work."[141]

Creator-to-Creator Tip #27
Strive for improvement, not perfection.

---

* * *

Going from occasional hobby to full-time creator whose income relies on your own grit, motivation, and execution can be difficult. But it can also be an exciting challenge to keep you on your toes creatively.

If you are struggling with motivation, find someone or several people who can hold you accountable. Be public with your upcoming projects and continually make mini deadlines for yourself. Write down your goals and

---

141 Ibid

cross them off so you can visually see your progress. And then reward yourself when you have completed the project or task related to the project.

You should always strive for growth and to be that person who you can see a marked improvement over a few years' worth of content. Only when you feel like you're ready should you take the plunge into full-time. It'll be a lot of work, but the results might surprise you.

Chapter 12

Consistency Is Key; Authenticity, Even More So

How can I be a successful creator in the long run?

On the list of still-active YouTubers who have been around since the "Wild West," no rules, no monetization era of YouTube, Jenna Marbles (the online name of Jenna Mourey) is still a well-known name today.

She has been active for so long yet still successfully uploads and makes her living through weekly random comedy videos (spanning such subjects as putting two hundred fake nails on one nail[142] to prank calling

---

142 JennaMarbles. "Putting 200 Fake Nails On One Nail." YouTube video, 13:37. Posted [March 2018].

in sick to jobs she doesn't have[143] to making a "draw my life" video for her dogs[144]). How does she do this when so many others from that same era have long since stopped?

The simple answer? Consistency.

Jenna says, "I think consistency has a lot to do with it, not falling off or not posting. It's my livelihood, my life, so I post every week, even when I'm tired and don't feel like it or life's getting hard."[145]

Consistency can be tough to maintain, but consistency is key. She still, nearly without fail, uploads every single Wednesday.

For her, consistency means the day of the week, which is one of two kinds of consistency found in these creative endeavors. Many other people follow a similar rule of thumb; having a set day, or even set time, when your videos come out is a higher guarantee for an audience because they will be looking for it—kind of like serial-

143 JennaMarbles. "Prank Calling In Sick From Jobs I Don't Have." YouTube video, 10:36. Posted [September 2015].

144 JennaMarbles. "My Dogs Draw Their Lives." YouTube video, 4:31. Posted [July 2015].

145 SRU Rocket. "An Interview with Jenna Marbles." YouTube video, 5:55. Posted [September 2018].

ized shows on network television. That is mostly what consistency will mean in this chapter.

But consistency could also mean consistent quality. Some channels come out with content more sporadically, but whenever they do, the amount of time needed to put the video together is obvious. This doesn't necessarily mean the daily or weekly posters have a lower quality of video. These two ideas of consistency could both work on the same channel as well.

Is one better than the other?

As a fan of many channels and podcasts with a variety of content, I do appreciate a schedule. Sometimes I look forward to a particular day of the week because, for example, it's Wednesday and I can't wait to see what Jenna came up with to watch while I take a study break. It's Friday, so that means the reaction to this particular show will be out. It's approximately 3 p.m. Pacific time, and that means this daily video should be out momentarily.

And do I get disappointed when content gets delayed or they have to take a week off? Sure. I'm only human.

But as a creator, taking more time between projects to dive into the research or editing or production value without the time crunch burden of posting on a certain day can be good. Instead of being held captive by a certain day of the week, you can use the power of social media to build up hype around the release of a project.

As a viewer, it can be similar to waiting for a movie or a new season of a show to release on a streaming service. There are still television shows on regular network television—Thursday comedy nights and primetime dramas, etc. There are still daily vloggers and weekly posters. It's comfortable and routine (and YouTube doesn't have any kind of time-shifting hurdle to cross because YouTube viewing is mostly time-shifted anyway).

But some streaming services take a year or so to create a new season of a show, with episode lengths however long they want, no commercials, all released at once to fans who have been waiting (let's be honest) since the second they finished the previous season.

Some creators post once a month, or a few times a month. Viewers might not even know the video is coming until it is posted (or they might have a day's warning once it's up on Patreon for advance viewing and the creator is satisfied with the final product). But they've subscribed for a reason, and they come in droves anyway.

Is one type of consistency or the other better?

Do you take longer to create something or put something out for the sake of your audience?

I think entertainment in general is going the way of the higher-value, sporadic content. Let me reiterate, however, that some people need a strict schedule. Pressure makes diamonds and all that. Having a contract with the audience to post something on a certain day can be what some people need to be creative.

Consistency by means of a schedule is still not a bad idea when you're starting out and trying to build an audience. Video marketing expert Sean Cannell says consistency is the key to success on YouTube for several reasons, including you will build trust with your audience, your audience has more chances to give you feedback, you get more practice as you learn how to create videos (the more you make, the better you get), and the YouTube algorithm likes consistency.[146]

---

146 Cannell, Sean. "Why Consistency is the Key to Growing your YouTube Channel." *LinkedIn.* October 16, 2018.

But it's not just consistency that keeps Jenna going. She thinks the secret to her success, and the success of her YouTube contemporaries, boils down to what this book has been trying to say.

She says, "I think also those people started at a time on YouTube when you couldn't make money and most people didn't know that you could or didn't ever dream that it was a possibility. So it's the organic wanting to make something and share it that I think drives people to create longer and stay consistent and be on the platform for longer."[147]

In other words, you're creatively fulfilled. You're not in it to make money or become famous.

Where have I heard that before?

Creator-to-Creator Tip #28
Purely wanting to make something and share it can lead to consistency and spending more time as a creator.

It can be hard, though, to consistently put things out there every single week. Missteps are bound to occur, and you have no way to know in advance how the audi-

---

147 SRU Rocket. "An Interview with Jenna Marbles." YouTube video, 5:55. Posted [September 2018].

ence will receive your content. These missteps could be diverging from your normal content to a new topic, trying a different style of presenting content than before, like skits or voiceover, or perhaps touching a topic that is controversial and drawing in more negative attention from outside your normal audience.

If this happens, make a note. See where the negativity is coming from. Is it your audience or outside? With your audience, maybe talk to some consistent commenters or patrons. If they support you, they will be honest and tell you what they didn't like. With outsiders, it's up to you whether you continue with this kind of content. Everything you do gives you more information to help you get better in the future.

Remember the previous chapter and how Ian likes to see how a creator evolves? That's a positive thing. It's okay if your first video is awful. The more you post, the better you become at not just creating videos but coming up with content and fielding an audience.

Even though she's been making videos for a long time, Jenna still doesn't have a clue whether something will go viral.

She says, "I never know, ever, if something is going to be popular—if people are going to like it or hate it. Sometimes whatever I think people are going to like, they hate. And sometimes, when I think something is boring and stupid and about nothing, it resonates with people. I've been making videos for seven years, and I couldn't tell you, honestly. I have no idea what's going to resonate with people. In terms of making something go viral, I have no clue, none."[148]

The most important thing is to just keep creating and putting yourself out there because something might take off. Even so, that's not the most important part of creating content. Did you enjoy making it? That's what counts.

Creator-to-Creator Tip #29
If you choose a weekly schedule and you're afraid you will end up in a rut, keep a running list of video ideas, whether they are internet challenges—though successful challenge videos need to keep timing in mind—or a broad topic or scraps of a script.

Jenna attributes a big part of her success to authenticity. People are attracted to the authenticity of internet

---

148 Patel, Deep. "YouTube Superstar Jenna Marbles Reveals the Secrets to Her Success." *HuffPost*. April 10, 2017.

creators because of the homespun nature that still permeates some longer-lived channels.

She says, "There are a lot of teenagers and early-twenties people consuming online entertainment. They have all this information at their fingertips on their phones, and they've already been exposed to television, and there's something about the internet that's just so authentically real. People are looking for that. They're actively searching for that."[149]

YouTube is just one of the many places where people can get a real look into someone's life, the mundane, the simple. Jenna says, "I watch people organize their kitchen drawers and go grocery shopping. And I don't know why. It's just infinitely fascinating. And it keeps people wanting to consume online media because it seems far more real than a production set on a television show."[150]

Livestreams and behind-the-scenes show the real work that goes into a video. There might be an entire room dedicated to creating content—one wall might be the podcast setup, and the opposite wall is a set for some videos. It's just someone's living room with a digital camera and some lamps, showing what the people

149 Ibid
150 Ibid

on camera are seeing. It draws back the curtain and, instead of shattering an illusion, it brings more clarity. And for some people, it brings inspiration.

I've definitely had this thought before: "They live in a dorm and literally just set up their webcam and bought a small lamp to light their face. They have 20,000 subscribers and a Patreon. I could do that too."

The quote about watching people go shopping brings up the idea that everyone is living their own life that is as complicated and mundane as yours. It also brings a connection between yourself and your audience. You probably go shopping with your roommate or your partner or a friend. When you vlog a shopping trip, you are saying to your audience: "Tag along, and you can be my friend too!"

This is how Jenna has lasted successfully for as long as she has—being real with an adapting and growing audience. She says, "I think I just do my best to grow with my audience, and not try to pretend I'm something that I'm not...I'm a grown adult. People who started watching me when I was twenty-three—they just grew up with me. It feels real. It is real. And I think that some of it has to do with growing up and not pretending to not grow up. It's just authenticity."[151]

She doesn't do the same things over and over, and she takes audience suggestions for videos. She engages with her audience and recognizes them for who they are, just as they see her for who she is. Her weekly videos sometimes consist of her reacting to memes or compilation videos of her content created by her audience. As of this writing, she has nearly twenty million subscribers, many of whom have been around for years.

Creator-to-Creator Tip #30
"Be yourself. Figure out what your voice is and use it. Say it, and unapologetically be yourself. But also engage with people. So if you're problematic and someone's like, "Hey, you're being really problematic," then take that advice. Understand what constructive criticism is."[152]

According to Jenna, there are two pillars of success on YouTube—consistency and authenticity.

Be yourself, be an authentic personality consistently through your videos. Pay attention to your audience because once you have a following, it's not just you

151 Patel, Deep. "YouTube Superstar Jenna Marbles Reveals the Secrets to Her Success." *HuffPost.* April 10, 2017.

152 Ibid

anymore. It's a two-sided relationship, and if you stop posting suddenly with no explanation, they might not come back. Find that balance, and your audience will appreciate you for owning up to mistakes as much as sticking to your guns on a topic.

When you receive constructive criticism from your audience, start by listening to your patrons and people who have been there the longest. They will know you best; you might be blind to your own shortcomings and need that outside perspective.

Know the difference between negative comments and constructive criticism. How many people are saying the same thing? If someone says they liked your lighting better last week, and fifty people like that comment, that's constructive criticism. I think you can probably come up with an example of a negative comment on your own. And if changing your lighting goes against your normal setup, there's a point in favor of consistency.

You also need to manage your expectations. Jenna says, "When I started on the internet, there was no viable internet career path, really, in terms of YouTube. There was no such thing as setting out to be an internet star. But I think if anyone is setting out with that intention, it's not going to end up that great. You might end up with some disappointments. But I think setting out to do something that you think is fun, and can be rewarding in the future, and is an awesome way to spend your time and share your thoughts: that's the way to go, rather than setting out to be some internet star."[153]

Along with authenticity, if all you have is a phone camera and an internet connection, that might be all you need to create something. Jenna says, "Because all that matters is that you're saying something that hits some nerve or resonates with people. It doesn't matter if you've got good sound and lighting. It doesn't matter at all."[154]

It's all about you, your voice, your thoughts, your words. Sure, it might be nice to have a good setup, but that isn't required right off the bat. If all you have right now is your phone and iMovie and you haven't made videos before, start with that. Don't buy fancy editing software or a camera unless you think it is worth the investment. That might take a few months. It all depends on what you want to do with your channel.

153 SRU Rocket. "An Interview with Jenna Marbles." YouTube video, 5:55. Posted [September 2018].
154 Patel, Deep. "YouTube Superstar Jenna Marbles Reveals the Secrets to Her Success." *HuffPost*. April 10, 2017.

* * *

There is more than one path to success. Consistency is one of those paths.

Part of Jenna's brand, besides uploading every single Wednesday, is filming, editing, and uploading on the same day. That's the one thing she wishes she could have changed about her YouTube path, but she hasn't stopped yet!

I can understand not wanting to change her brand this far into her YouTube journey. Perhaps keeping everything in such a tight timeline helps with her creative process. If she had unlimited time, she might not get it done.

You can try this method if you want—it could be seen as an extreme form of self-motivation!

However, I for one can't imagine coming up with a new idea every single week and filming, editing, and posting all in one day. That's not in my mindset in the least. I'm a bit of a perfectionist, and I don't want to rush art. So when I make something, for the most part, it's because I want it to happen.

That doesn't mean there isn't something
comes to considering consistency. Som
that, in order to keep creating, becaus
have that consistency, they might stop

Remember, there are two types of consi
and quantity. It is possible to have both
YouTube likes quantity, but entertainr
seems to lean more toward quality.

No matter what you do in terms of cor
ticity should absolutely remain.

Chapter 13

Keeping It Small

Can I still be successful if I don't create full-time?

Sometimes you don't have to have the biggest channel or have the most views to feel successful on YouTube. It doesn't even have to be your full-time job for you to love it. For Nathaniel Wayne, the Council of Geeks YouTube channel is an income supplement and a reliable, regular creative outlet—and he's fine with that!

His four videos a week, mostly reviews of movies and television and "geeky rambles" about whatever fandoms he is interested in as well as related topics in media, scratch his creative itch and give him a connection with a fellow geeky audience. These videos are usually around ten to fifteen minutes but can be as long as twenty or thirty if the topic is large enough or he has a lot to say!

In keeping with the last chapter, one factor in his success could be consistency. He uploads multiple times in a week and has several ongoing series within these videos (such as his "Overdue *Doctor Who* Reviews").

He is also a crew of one (minus the guy who makes his thumbnails) and taught himself all he knows about video production. Clocking in at 37,000 subscribers at the time of this writing, he is not the biggest channel in this book.

But his goal isn't to be the biggest channel. Once he found out he enjoyed just rambling at the camera, he says, "Any success that I've found since then is by accident rather than design."[155]

Recalling the unpredictable nature of the YouTube algorithm, which controls what is recommended or trending for individual viewers, it can be a challenge keeping up with all the spoken or unspoken changes to the algorithm "rules" and deciding whether your content has what it takes to have your videos trending.

Some factors the algorithm may take into consideration include what tags you put on your video, the title, the

---

155 Wayne, Nathaniel in discussion with the author, January 31, 2019.

content, or the time the video uploads. To be trending on YouTube is like winning the lottery, except much rarer, and even those who have been on the site for a long time are still trying to figure out how it works.

For some people, constantly looking at analytics and reevaluating the strategies might be fun and considered part of the game. But not for Nathaniel.

"I can look at my analytics and I can get some broad strokes, but I'm not the kind of person who can break stuff down...and reconfigure what I'm doing to maximize clicks."[156] And "I'm at the point where I'm big enough where, theoretically, somebody with a different sort of mindset than me would start charting the trends and doing stuff like that, I don't even want to do that now because I'm afraid it would suck the fun out of it."[157]

Creator Need-to-Know Definitions:
Analytics – In social media, this is information gathered about a certain post, photo, video, etc. Examples include demographic information of viewers, general ratios of likes to dislikes, number of shares, or how long people watch each video. Many social media platforms have analytics tools that provide this information, gathered since the beginning of the social media account, displayed in charts and graphs. Because of the amount of data and endless

---

156 Wayne, Nathaniel in discussion with the author, January 31, 2019.
157 Ibid

possibilities of tracking and comparison between different videos, reading analytics can take some getting used to.

Clicks – In this sense, literally a person clicking (or tapping on a phone) onto your videos. Another way to say this is number of views; the more clicks, the more eyeballs on your video. To maximize clicks, compare specific videos or one month to the next. If the number of views, comments, or subscribers went up (or down), determine what you changed.

Nathaniel proves that you don't have to be a huge YouTuber to enjoy all the benefits of having a channel, especially having an audience. In fact, being small might be a bit of an advantage in his case. A smaller audience means fewer comments, which makes it more reasonable to read all of them and give specific replies or hearts. Creator hearts are YouTube's way of indicating the video creator specifically liked the comment.

He says, "I personally really love my audience, and I think a fair amount of that I can level to the fact that I curate my comments and actively moderate them, which is annoying and it's a lot of work, but it does foster an atmosphere I'm happy with."[158]

By curating and moderating, he is looking for intentionally vile comments and removing them. This way,

---

158 Ibid

with some disappointments. But I think setting out to do something that you think is fun, and can be rewarding in the future, and is an awesome way to spend your time and share your thoughts: that's the way to go, rather than setting out to be some internet star."[153]

Along with authenticity, if all you have is a phone camera and an internet connection, that might be all you need to create something. Jenna says, "Because all that matters is that you're saying something that hits some nerve or resonates with people. It doesn't matter if you've got good sound and lighting. It doesn't matter at all."[154]

It's all about you, your voice, your thoughts, your words. Sure, it might be nice to have a good setup, but that isn't required right off the bat. If all you have right now is your phone and iMovie and you haven't made videos before, start with that. Don't buy fancy editing software or a camera unless you think it is worth the investment. That might take a few months. It all depends on what you want to do with your channel.

153 SRU Rocket. "An Interview with Jenna Marbles." YouTube video, 5:55. Posted [September 2018].

154 Patel, Deep. "YouTube Superstar Jenna Marbles Reveals the Secrets to Her Success." *HuffPost.* April 10, 2017.

* * *

There is more than one path to success. Consistency is one of those paths.

Part of Jenna's brand, besides uploading every single Wednesday, is filming, editing, and uploading on the same day. That's the one thing she wishes she could have changed about her YouTube path, but she hasn't stopped yet!

I can understand not wanting to change her brand this far into her YouTube journey. Perhaps keeping everything in such a tight timeline helps with her creative process. If she had unlimited time, she might not get it done.

You can try this method if you want—it could be seen as an extreme form of self-motivation!

However, I for one can't imagine coming up with a new idea every single week and filming, editing, and posting all in one day. That's not in my mindset in the least. I'm a bit of a perfectionist, and I don't want to rush art. So when I make something, for the most part, it's because I want it to happen.

That doesn't mean there isn't something there when it comes to considering consistency. Some people need that, in order to keep creating, because if they don't have that consistency, they might stop altogether.

Remember, there are two types of consistency—quality and quantity. It is possible to have both on one channel. YouTube likes quantity, but entertainment, in general, seems to lean more toward quality.

No matter what you do in terms of consistency, authenticity should absolutely remain.

Chapter 13

Keeping It Small

Can I still be successful if I don't create full-time?

Sometimes you don't have to have the biggest channel or have the most views to feel successful on YouTube. It doesn't even have to be your full-time job for you to love it. For Nathaniel Wayne, the Council of Geeks YouTube channel is an income supplement and a reliable, regular creative outlet—and he's fine with that!

His four videos a week, mostly reviews of movies and television and "geeky rambles" about whatever fandoms he is interested in as well as related topics in media, scratch his creative itch and give him a connection with a fellow geeky audience. These videos are usually around ten to fifteen minutes but can be as long as twenty or thirty if the topic is large enough or he has a lot to say!

In keeping with the last chapter, one factor in his success could be consistency. He uploads multiple times in a week and has several ongoing series within these videos (such as his "Overdue *Doctor Who* Reviews").

He is also a crew of one (minus the guy who makes his thumbnails) and taught himself all he knows about video production. Clocking in at 37,000 subscribers at the time of this writing, he is not the biggest channel in this book.

But his goal isn't to be the biggest channel. Once he found out he enjoyed just rambling at the camera, he says, "Any success that I've found since then is by accident rather than design."[155]

Recalling the unpredictable nature of the YouTube algorithm, which controls what is recommended or trending for individual viewers, it can be a challenge keeping up with all the spoken or unspoken changes to the algorithm "rules" and deciding whether your content has what it takes to have your videos trending.

Some factors the algorithm may take into consideration include what tags you put on your video, the title, the

---

155 Wayne, Nathaniel in discussion with the author, January 31, 2019.

content, or the time the video uploads. To be trending on YouTube is like winning the lottery, except much rarer, and even those who have been on the site for a long time are still trying to figure out how it works.

For some people, constantly looking at analytics and reevaluating the strategies might be fun and considered part of the game. But not for Nathaniel.

"I can look at my analytics and I can get some broad strokes, but I'm not the kind of person who can break stuff down...and reconfigure what I'm doing to maximize clicks."[156] And "I'm at the point where I'm big enough where, theoretically, somebody with a different sort of mindset than me would start charting the trends and doing stuff like that, I don't even want to do that now because I'm afraid it would suck the fun out of it."[157]

Creator Need-to-Know Definitions:
Analytics – In social media, this is information gathered about a certain post, photo, video, etc. Examples include demographic information of viewers, general ratios of likes to dislikes, number of shares, or how long people watch each video. Many social media platforms have analytics tools that provide this information, gathered since the beginning of the social media account, displayed in charts and graphs. Because of the amount of data and endless

156 Wayne, Nathaniel in discussion with the author, January 31, 2019.
157 Ibid

possibilities of tracking and comparison between different videos, reading analytics can take some getting used to.

Clicks – In this sense, literally a person clicking (or tapping on a phone) onto your videos. Another way to say this is number of views; the more clicks, the more eyeballs on your video. To maximize clicks, compare specific videos or one month to the next. If the number of views, comments, or subscribers went up (or down), determine what you changed.

Nathaniel proves that you don't have to be a huge YouTuber to enjoy all the benefits of having a channel, especially having an audience. In fact, being small might be a bit of an advantage in his case. A smaller audience means fewer comments, which makes it more reasonable to read all of them and give specific replies or hearts. Creator hearts are YouTube's way of indicating the video creator specifically liked the comment.

He says, "I personally really love my audience, and I think a fair amount of that I can level to the fact that I curate my comments and actively moderate them, which is annoying and it's a lot of work, but it does foster an atmosphere I'm happy with."[158]

By curating and moderating, he is looking for intentionally vile comments and removing them. This way,

---

158 Ibid

people can be free to voice their opinion in his comment sections—a conversation among a Council of Geeks, if you will.

As he says at the end of his videos, "You're the council, and I'm just running the meetings!" He actively encourages his audience to discuss, and while that doesn't make him unique among creators, that makes his channel feel more like a community and a place for free discussion.

He says, "I know there are certainly plenty of creators out there who basically ignore their comment sections completely because it's a total mess and they just go by views and that's kind of it. I like the level of interaction I feel like I've been able to foster on my channel, and I find that very fulfilling."[159]

It doesn't hurt that he has a Patreon as well for an even more personal experience with some of his followers. He says, "So what Patreon is great for is for allowing an easy platform for the people who believe that what I do has value, to be able to support me, and for me to tap in more directly with people that are willing to actually support me on that level."[160]

---

159 Wayne, Nathaniel in discussion with the author, January 31, 2019.
160 Ibid

They can answer polls and give feedback a little more directly than through a comment section, and they can also offer suggestions for what to cover on the channel through certain perks. Patreon also gives him more reliable supplemental income, since his YouTube income might come and go due to what he is reviewing (such as a huge uptick when *Doctor Who* is on the air), and it can be hard to plan what the algorithm, or the casual audience, likes.

Pop Culture Plug

Doctor Who is the world's longest-running sci-fi television series, first airing in 1963. It follows the adventures of a time-traveling alien called The Doctor, who changes bodies and personalities upon death (how the series maintained its longevity—literally recast your main character every few years!). With multiple television spin-offs and quite the collection of audio dramas and novels, there is much to dive into in terms of content for a channel.

To someone starting out on YouTube, he offers this advice: "Never expect to get big. Like, ever. Whatever you do, do it the way you want to do it and be sure you're having fun doing it because the odds are that for a very long time, effectively nobody will be watching, and you are doing it for yourself. If you get hung up on the idea of trying to go viral ...when you're just starting out, all you're gonna do is set yourself up for disappointment."[161]

If I consistently added videos to my YouTube channel and pursued it as more of a dedicated hobby, I would want a channel like Council of Geeks. I wouldn't mind having a small audience able to discuss their favorite things in a close-knit setting.

But this all means nothing if you are not satisfied with what you are creating.

As previously stated, doing something you enjoy should be the fundamental motivation behind content creation. If you aren't doing it for yourself on some level, eventually, you will stop enjoying it and then possibly have less motivation.

Keep asking yourself, are you fulfilled?

Creator-to-Creator Tip #31
Never expect to get big.

* * *

---

161 Ibid

Starting small isn't a bad thing. Keeping it small and not going full-time may not be a bad idea either. Having a close connection with an audience makes it easier to interact with more of them directly, and because of this, I think it might be easier to maintain authenticity with a smaller audience.

When you lack authenticity, your audience might be able to tell and then leave, and then where would you be? The smaller the audience, the more impact you will feel with each lost subscriber.

Keep in mind no one becomes successful overnight. Not everyone setting out to become successful becomes successful. Especially in this online world, it can be difficult to tell what will be successful and what won't. Knowing analytics can get you so far, but that can also be difficult to maintain on your own and tedious to constantly monitor.

But if you start by doing your project for yourself, and then doing it for your audience, any success that comes your way will be well-earned.

Chapter 14

YouTube And Musicians

Is YouTube a good place for musicians?

Peter Hollens is revolutionizing what it means to be a musician.

He is a classically trained singer who has slowly built up an audience on YouTube around his pop and pop culture-inspired a cappella (voice only) covers of songs. He wasn't the first musician to make a mark on YouTube in the early 2010s.

However, by following the examples of the success stories and music output of other channels that came before him (such as the music covers brought to life on Kurt Hugo Schneider's channel through unconventional instruments and constant collaborations), he found inspiration to create.

He used what he already knew from his time as a producer and sound engineer recording random college a cappella groups for $25 an hour, and then "turned the mic on [himself]."[162]

He says, "I created my fanbase out of thin air, and it was done exclusively for the first five years on YouTube. They've provided the best set of tools for creators to do that, and I've been absolutely fortunate enough to create a business utilizing their infrastructure...Being able to release something and then release it to five million people is so powerful."[163]

The five million is a bit of a random number—he has over two million subscribers and his videos get anywhere from under one million to his highest at eighteen million—but the intent still stands. Releasing something you created to one of the biggest platforms on the internet is a bit of a scary leap, but it can be powerful at the same time.

But releasing music on YouTube takes a little careful planning. It's not just about releasing the music; if that

162 Ross, Danny. "How Peter Hollens Changed The Music Industry From His Living Room." *Forbes.* March 8, 2017.

163 Zellner, Xander. "Peter Hollens, A Cappella Breakout Star, Talks First Chart-Topping Album "Legendary Folk Songs"." *Billboard.* June 29, 2018.

was the case, he could have used a service like Sound-Cloud to share his originals.

YouTube is a video sharing platform, and with that comes the almost necessary visual aspect of the final product. There's no reason a talented musician can't come up with a way to make a video if that is their goal. You can teach yourself how to do that; you already know how to sing.

Your video could just be you from a few different angles in a striking environment like a church or an ornate stage. You could travel to some different locations, film it in a studio, or add crazy props and costumes. If it's a cappella, like Peter's videos, if one person is singing multiple parts, recorded separately, each of those clips can appear on the screen at the same time—a choir of one. It depends on the content of the song itself, and how much of a crew and budget you have to invest.

Also, if it is a cover, you might need to get legal permission through licensing the use of the song, especially if you want to sell the audio or profit from your video!

But no matter what the song is, if you want to release it to a YouTube audience, you need to consider the video accompanying the audio. Peter says, "Content is the king, music video is the queen, and those two things need to be married. Otherwise, you don't have a product. I don't believe in an album anymore, everything needs to be a single."[164] Putting the work into a single song and accompanying video makes each release even more special.

* * *

As the channel grew, Peter began to bring more people on to help edit the sound to make the best product he could. He's not doing everything alone anymore, but he is still an independent musician thanks to his audience and Patreon.

He says, "The only thing that matters in a music career is your community. I believe that Patreon is the first company that has truly understood where we're going in this 'Creator Revolution.'"[165] That's his way of saying what I've been looking at all along—independent and audience-funded entrepreneur creators functioning through the internet as their main means of distribution are on the rise.

---

164 Ross, Danny. "How Peter Hollens Changed The Music Industry From His Living Room." *Forbes.* March 8, 2017.

165 Ibid

Patreon, in part, has made it possible. It's about the content and the people behind the content, a push toward encouraging people to make their living doing things that at one point were considered subpar ways to make money, like being a musician. Viewers want to support the creators they like and have more control over their entertainment than ever before. And the creators feel like they are getting something for pouring their souls into their work.

Let me say it again—Thank you, Jack Conte!

Peter did get a lucky break, though. He collaborated with another YouTube breakout musician named Lindsey Stirling, a talented violinist who dances while she plays. Their first video in 2012 was an arrangement of the main theme from the video game *Skyrim*, and it quadrupled Peter's fanbase. He has made a point of collaborating with other musicians ever since, whether they are fellow YouTubers or more mainstream.

Collaboration on YouTube can be viewed in a few different ways. The first way is like Peter and Lindsey Stirling. Peter benefitted from Lindsey's popularity and gained subscribers. The second way is the opposite, like what Peter sometimes does now—help someone smaller gain a little more audience.

The third way is when a few YouTubers are friends and are more equal in terms of audience and collaborate because they want to. All can be done for fun and with no politicking, though. If you are a brand-new creator, I would wait until you had a few thousand subscribers before reaching out (like through a business email listed on the YouTube channel or messaging on a social media account) to do a collaboration. Networking with other creators can be invaluable, not just for collaboration but help and support, especially if the other creator has been a YouTuber longer.

Creator-to-Creator Tip #32

The cool thing about technology is creators do not have to be in the same room to collaborate. They can record things separately, or if it is more of a conversation, record the conversation itself, like a video chat. But it is easy to tell when creators are in the same room and they are just enjoying each other's creative spirits, or they are bouncing off each other's humor. Collaboration can be fun!

Collaboration does not just have to occur between creators in the same field, like two musicians, comedians, or fandom experts. Two creators from different "genres" can collaborate as a means of cross-promotion. For example, someone who writes or covers music could collaborate with someone who does makeup or other tutorials that require background music.

Peter's view of other musicians makes him stand out from others in a creative field. He says, "I started viewing artists on YouTube as peers, not as competitors. The second an artist can change their mind from looking at it about making money, to helping others and doing it because you love it, it's insane how much more successful you'll be. I always give more than I get. Always. From the first penny in gross revenue, I'll usually split everything in perpetuity. So it's not about money; it's about relationship-building, transparency. The relationship you have for decades is much more important than a one-off where you try to siphon a few more dollars from somebody else."[166]

He isn't just using someone's name, like Lindsey Stirling or, say, David Archuleta, for clicks. He genuinely wants to collaborate with these talented people to share a love of music, a love of fandom, a love of creation with a combined audience. And isn't that what creating should be all about?

Just because he made his start on YouTube doesn't mean he stayed there. He has recorded many albums, with a folk song album in 2018 becoming a *Billboard* No. 1.

He is also looking to the future of his brand and started The Hollens Creator Academy. With these online courses, creators can learn how to make a living doing

166 Ross, Danny. "How Peter Hollens Changed The Music Industry From His Living Room." *Forbes.* March 8, 2017.

what they love. Peter will be able "to teach people how they can do what I do. Through the experience I've gained over the past decade, I am excited to show creators how they can pursue their dreams and support themselves at the same time."[167]

These video courses teach about entrepreneurship and navigating the digital space, a great thing for newcomers to this field. He is taking what he knows and what he is passionate about and giving insight into what it means to be a creator, urging emerging artists to join "The Creator Revolution." He says, "I am extremely passionate about helping other people make a living in the digital sphere."[168]

His introductory video for the courses sums up many of the points I have hit on so far in this book, including fighting against the "starving artist" label.[169] This Creator Revolution inspired me to write this book.

Creator-to-Creator Tip #33
View others in your field not as competitors but as peers and potential collaborators.

---

167 Potts, Ricky. "Artist Interview: 1-on-1 with Peter Hollens." *Ricky Lee Potts.* June 2017.

168 Ibid

169 HOLLENS CREATOR ACADEMY. "How to Make a Living Online - Peter Hollens." YouTube video, 5:18. Posted [December 2017].

You don't have to be tied to a record label be successful. Peter knows this through experience. That wasn't who he wanted to become, so he shaped his life to fit what he wanted.

He says, "I quickly realized that someone like myself should never have anyone telling them what to do. I'm a digital brand. I can create an entire career never leaving my cul-de-sac in Eugene, Oregon... Once you have control of something and you build it yourself, it's very hard to relinquish...Going on the road two hundred days a year is not going to make me a good father and a good husband, and I don't think musicians need to do that anymore."[170]

Even though he is busy with the Creator Academy, he still puts out new music videos on YouTube, because if his primary content will be music videos, that is the best way to get that content to his audience.

He says, "I have been able to foster a community on the platform that has accelerated my career in ways that I never would have imagined."[171] Being tied to the right

170 Ross, Danny. "How Peter Hollens Changed The Music Industry From His Living Room." *Forbes.* March 8, 2017.

171 Potts, Ricky. "Artist Interview: 1-on-1 with Peter Hollens." *Ricky Lee Potts.* June 2017.

record label is not the only way to become a famous musician anymore and is certainly not the way to become a fulfilled artist.

As a musician myself, it is interesting to see this worldview, especially from someone who made their start on YouTube. You don't need to release albums. You don't need super high production value, just high enough to meet your standards. You don't need to fight against similar artists on the platform or exploit them for views. You can just make a video. It can be, dare I say, fun?

Well, this is certainly inspiring me to get up and create something—after all, YouTube musicians have been slowly fueling my desire to make a music video... eventually.

* * *

YouTube can be a wonderful place for musicians, full of freedom and collaboration and expression, sharing your gift and your talent because *you* want to. Creating a video just adds something more to the final product.

This is the most important takeaway from Peter's experiences: "I don't want to be some famous millionaire; that's not my prerogative. I want to create something

that's meaningful to my fanbase, meaningful to me."[172]
Peter is absolutely a creator who embodies the spirit of
"fulfilled, not famous"!

Others besides him are still genuinely creating for the
sake of creating. They are using their talents to share
something beautiful with the world.

And you can join them too.

172 Ross, Danny. "How Peter Hollens Changed The Music Industry From
    His Living Room." *Forbes*. March 8, 2017.

Chapter 15

The Art of the Video Essay

What is a video essay and when would I make one?

YouTube has led to different sub-genres of videos. There are theory videos, how-to videos, parody videos, music videos, vlogs, etc., many of which are created by the other YouTubers found in this book.

But one sub-genre interesting to me as an academic is the video essay.

While far from being the first person to create a video essay, Lindsay Ellis has been making them popular through her own particular brand of snark and wit as she expertly talks about franchises and characters we all know and love.

So what exactly is a video essay?

Lindsay says they are pretty much what they sound like, but "there's a misconception that a video essay is just a long ramble edited. They're incorrectly defined. To me, a video essay is an essay. It has a thesis. It has a central argument and supporting evidence."[173]

Video essays are crafted as carefully as a written academic essay and can appeal to all sorts of people in the way a written essay might not.

The key is that the visual elements are essential in creating a product that can draw in viewers; a video essay uses *video*, not just a narrative.

She says, "Video essays are popular on YouTube right now specifically for visual media, and that's where I personally think their strengths are best applied. It's a new type of film writing where instead of describing a scene, you are able to use elements of the scene to help strengthen whatever argument you're making."[174]

Lindsay is an example of someone who took what they learned in school and adapted it to the new platform; she has degrees in film from NYU and USC. A film

---

173 Graham, Kathryn. "Kathryn Graham has a Conversation with Lindsay Ellis—Part I." *TV Writer.* January 9, 2019.

174 Ibid

critic means something a little different on YouTube, and video essays are a huge part of that.

She doesn't just look into pop culture, though her essays on *The Hobbit*, different Disney films such as the *Beauty and the Beast* remake and *The Hunchback of Notre Dame*, *Transformers*, and *The Phantom of the Opera* are a big chunk of her output. In these essays, she discusses many things—production, story themes, problems with characters or writing, connections to the source material, and, in *The Hobbit* series, the negative experience of the actors and the effect on the New Zealand film industry.[175]

Her latest videos, as of this writing, were less about these topics and about things like Death of the Author (a concept meaning the creator's intent does not matter after the final product is released), product placement, and manufacturing authenticity on YouTube.

Video essays don't *have* to be about film and television—the audiovisual nature of videos lends itself to being the right medium to talk about film and television. They can be about anything you can center a good argument around and a topic you can cover in twenty to forty minutes or so.

175 Ellis, Lindsay. "The Hobbit: The Desolation of Warners (Part 3/2)." YouTube video, 30:37. Posted [April 2018].

As with other YouTubers, she has to be smart in not just the topic of the videos but who she pairs with for sponsorships. Because of this, her scripts are carefully written.

Lindsay says, "We're very careful with our words. You have to be. The trick is to make it seem informal, but all our words are chosen very carefully. Because a lot of words that are very commonplace in academia you can't use on YouTube like 'hegemony,' 'patriarchy,' or 'feminist framework.' So you have to write around those. It has to appear informal and accessible while still getting your point across."[176]

It's a balance to remain informal for the casual viewer who may not have as wide a knowledge in film storytelling and critique as Lindsay, but also to get her point across on possibly touchy topics sponsors do not want to be associated with. This can make the writing process a little long and difficult, but sometimes balance must be taken into account if you still want to publish on YouTube and have ads and sponsorships.

---

176 Graham, Kathryn. "Kathryn Graham has a Conversation with Lindsay Ellis—Part I." *TV Writer.* January 9, 2019.

She partners with a long-time friend, Angelina Meegan, to brainstorm ideas, write the scripts, and do research. And as anyone who has created any kind of thesis or research project knows, the research is where some of the most important work for the final product happens.

Lindsay says, "A lot of times the thesis will change based on the research. A lot of YouTubers obviously don't have any professional journalism background. When you start with a thesis, you're trying to find supporting evidence for it. But a lot of times you'll find, 'Hmm, maybe when I first came up with this idea, I was not educated on a certain sect.' A lot of YouTubers tend to fall down this hole of ignoring that and only focusing on evidence that supports their argument. The tricky thing there is being open to your thesis changing or being completely invalid to where you need to trash the project."[177]

She has noticed that when emotions behind the argument run high, there is an element of timing in terms of video relevance; the videos do better in terms of views and the algorithm. However, because of a stronger connection to the topic and need for timeliness, less research is involved.

---

177 Graham, Kathryn. "Kathryn Graham has a Conversation with Lindsay Ellis—Part I." *TV Writer.* January 9, 2019.

Lindsay cites her take on the *Beauty and the Beast* remake as one such video. "We already know everything about Disney's *Beauty and the Beast*. We don't need a lot of research. It's just pure vitriol."[178] In that essay, an oft-occurring phrase in her dialogue was, "Thanks, I hate it!" delivered with a sweet smile as she went through each of the problems she had with the movie as well as some details of behind-the-scenes Disney executives and movie-making history that helped frame why this movie came out when it did.[179]

It's not just the carefully edited scripts that makes YouTube not always the best place for video essays. It is also how YouTube and its algorithm works. It likes consistency, and that isn't always possible with videos that can take months to make, on varying topics, of varying lengths. However, as I said previously, for the audience consistency in the quality of videos makes the inconsistent uploading schedule a non-argument.

This makes what Lindsay is doing right now and where she will go in the future uncertain. Even though the quality of the videos on YouTube is going up overall, the platform itself just isn't catching up and might not be

178 Ibid

179 Ellis, Lindsay. "That Time Disney Remade Beauty and the Beast." YouTube video, 36:52. Posted [July 2018].

sustainable for some people. Only time will tell if You-Tube makes the adjustments needed to support not just the daily or weekly creators, but the long-form, sporadic creators as well.

Luckily, at least for now, there are Patreon patrons, sponsorships, and almost 800,000 subscribers to keep Lindsay going. She also has a successful web series with PBS called *It's Lit!* which breaks down ideas about writing, books, and famous novels. It will be exciting to see what her next video essays turn out to be.

* * *

Lindsay's advice for future video essayists is not to mimic others' voices but work to find your own. "Practice it. It's your first one. It's not going to be good. I think people need to learn to be okay with that. It's a process. It's like any skill. Most people will have a kernel of an idea of what their voice is going to be. This is a medium. It's not the same as prose. It's a process to find it. A lot of people that I now consider peers had such a learning curve. You need to figure out what you're good at and what your voice is."[180]

---

180 Graham, Kathryn. "A Conversation with Lindsay Ellis—Part II." *TV Writer.* January 16, 2019.

Personally, I think it would be fun to create a video essay. Thanks to YouTube, I have been looking at the film and television I consume in a different light. I pay attention to storytelling, consistency, and character development and growth the most since watching video essays. I especially enjoy watching things more than once and look for subtle details in callbacks, different writers, and clues in the music. I watch a lot of video essays, and I have a few ideas and started scripts floating around my digital files. Whether they see the light of day will depend on if I think I have a strong enough argument. I am by no means an expert in things like storytelling or film making, but that's where research comes in.

Creator-to-Creator Tip #34
It will take time to find your creative voice in this new medium, so practice.

---

* * *

Are you an academic who loves research but is sick of writing papers? You might want to try a video essay— just like a written essay but with fun audiovisual elements to back up your argument.

So pick your favorite movie and start picking it apart! Take notes when you watch, pay attention to characters, the setting, the costumes, or the music—whatever interests you. Do some research and look for trivia. Compare performances of actors in different shows or shot quality in different films by the same director. The possibilities are endless.

And you don't have to be an expert in film to make a video essay! As long as the care and attention are there, the argument is formed as clearly as a written essay, and the research is done, you will make a product you can be proud of—a YouTube-only kind of creation.

Chapter 16

Considering Unexpected Fame

What if I do get famous?

In Part I, we talked about using hot wings to get vulnerable interviewees.

In Part II, we discussed turning the desire to learn more about cooking into a full-time job making fictional treats.

Now we're in Part III, and I couldn't help adding another food-related channel. How could I resist looking into a series called *My Drunk Kitchen*?

It is what it sounds like—YouTuber Hannah Hart gets drunk and cooks (don't try this at home!). Even though that is what she is known for, there is so much more to her channel and experience. Her multiple years on the platform have shown her not just how one channel can grow but how to have a healthy and responsible approach to unexpected fame.

My Drunk Kitchen began in March 2011, when she wanted to reconnect with a friend by sending her a video of her making up a cooking show while drunk (the meal in question was a simple grilled cheese sandwich...with buttered bread but, in fact, no actual cheese).[181]

She then shared it with her friend via YouTube, and because it wasn't an unlisted video, anyone could see it. Imagine her surprise when it went viral, by the standards of the day—about 80,000 views (it's up to 4.3 million now!)!

It opened Hannah up to a whole new world of what she could be doing. She didn't even realize YouTube culture was a thing, that people were putting shows online and getting paid for it!

Once she saw people liked what she was doing, she made another and another. She says, "Then two-and-a-half weeks after that, I was like, 'I don't want to be known for being drunk,' so I made a video that wasn't about

---

181 MyHarto. "My Drunk Kitchen Ep. 1: Butter Yo Shit." YouTube video, 5:21. Posted [March 2011].

that."[182] But nothing was getting as many views as *My Drunk Kitchen*, so she stuck with that.

Remember Chapter 7 and the importance of consistency and wording in titles. Each episode of *My Drunk Kitchen* is labeled as such in the title of the video. Besides being organizational, it is also a way to drag in new viewers— doesn't that series title make you just a little curious?

"And that was it. I just enjoyed it more and more. It takes up more and more of your time. I took a plunge."[183] She wasn't sure when she decided she wanted this internet life to be a full-time thing, but she's definitely there now. It's, as she says, "the best job in the world."[184]

A big part of why it is the best job in the world is the community created around the channel. Hannah loves the community she has built, full of supportive and kind people who want to talk.

If YouTube were a house party, she says, "My channel is for the people who want to hang out in the kitchen.

182 Tiffany, Kaitlyn. "My Drunk Kitchen creator Hannah Hart on life as a YouTube star." *The Verge*. October 19, 2016.

183 Tiffany, Kaitlyn. "My Drunk Kitchen creator Hannah Hart on life as a YouTube star." *The Verge*. October 19, 2016.

184 Saxe, Lizzy. "How Do You Describe Hannah Hart's Career? It's Complicated." *Forbes*. November 28, 2018.

That's where I hang out when I'm at a party. If I'm at a house party, I go into the kitchen because it's a little bit quieter, you're still drinking, you're having fun, but it's kind of a space where you have good conversations. It's that quality that makes it more appealing than just the drinking and just the comedy, I think it's the intimacy."[185]

It's just her talking in her kitchen, so that does a lot to lower the mental barrier for entry to the viewer. It's comfortable; it's familiar. You feel like you're in the kitchen with her.

* * *

She wasn't expecting internet fame; no one is. Like we've seen, there is no way to predict how or when something will go viral. But what you do with that fame defines you as a person as well as an internet personality.

Hannah says, "[Internet fame] has changed my life completely in the way that it's given me a platform and a great deal of purpose and responsibility. It's kind of amazing because I am a de facto role model and public figure. I take that incredibly seriously, and so my job is to make the most out of my life and try to be as sincere

---

185 Tiffany, Kaitlyn. "My Drunk Kitchen creator Hannah Hart on life as a YouTube star." *The Verge*. October 19, 2016.

and sincerely happy and content as possible. It would be so disgraceful and disrespectful if I took an opportunity like this and I just wasted it on myself."[186]

Using your platform and your voice for good is one of the most important things you can do in a position of power and influence. The charity livestream for St. Jude's in Chapter 4 is far from the only example of a YouTuber raising money for a cause or bringing awareness to something that matters to the creator and should matter to the audience as well.

There can be a dark side to celebrity life, though. You can get caught up in the glamor of it all and focus on your outward appearance and image and worry less about what is important—yourself and your own growth.

Hannah's advice for this? "I feel like anyone who makes over six figures, just as an obligation, should go to therapy so they don't bring their money and their issues into the rest of the world. There are so many people who have so much power and have done so little personal development."[187]

186 Ibid
187 Tiffany, Kaitlyn. "My Drunk Kitchen creator Hannah Hart on life as a YouTube star." *The Verge*. October 19, 2016.

Unexpected fame can tear a person apart if unchecked, especially today, when the barrier for entry of being a successful influencer is low and the number of eyes on you at all times is high thanks to the ubiquity of social media. Having someone, therapist or otherwise, there to knock you down from a narcissistic high can save your public image.

Because of the less successful stories of those who let fame get away from them, these different stories of channel creation and audience growth are so special. The growth of a channel and a community over time is amazing when it is natural. This growth is a reflection and representation of the journey of not just the creator but the audience as well, as they learn together and progress through the years.

This was Hannah's experience. She says, "I think that one of the reasons that I'm so grateful for the channel and for the community and the way it's evolved to this point is that in 2011, it was still so not intentional and people didn't have goals of becoming a 'YouTube Star'...I think if your goal is to be famous, then I don't know if there's ever any amount of views that's going to be satisfying to you."[188]

---

188 Ibid

What makes her sad are those who care about just the views, viewing themselves as a failure if they don't get a million views right away as opposed to being grateful for this wide-reaching platform where they can share their art and their ideas.

You shouldn't aim for fame; you should aim for fulfillment!

Creator-to-Creator Tip #35
"The more self-knowledge, self-acceptance, and approval you can give to yourself as a creative, the better experience you're going to have. I'm not looking to be the number one YouTuber or the number one anything. I'm looking to maintain my creative career. So any day that I wake up and I still get a chance to do this? That's a good day."[189]

Creator-to-Creator Tip #36
Safety first! Be smart with what you choose to share online. Never post your phone number, your address, or personal email address. Create an email account just for your audience. Open a P.O. box so your audience can send you things. Keep identifying street signs and window views out of your shots. Do not reveal where you work (if YouTube is not yet your full-time job). Once you post something online, it is up there forever, and if audience members want to find you, they will find a way. Be careful, be smart, and report any harassment.

---

189 Saxe, Lizzy. "How Do You Describe Hannah Hart's Career? It's Complicated." *Forbes.* November 28, 2018.

Fame isn't the goal. The goal is to be creatively fulfilled, to use your platform for good, to make real connections, to learn something new.

But if you become famous because of what you do, that's not a bad thing. Keep yourself grounded and rooted in the real world. Act like a role model. Take breaks from your online presence. Talk to people about what you are feeling.

It is important to remember why you started doing it all in the first place. If you do that, you will make quite the mark on YouTube.

Chapter 17

Highlights of Creator Tips

By now you should have a better understanding of the YouTube space, a few ways to brainstorm channel topics (and maybe even an idea or two), and the knowledge of some things to expect and keep in mind once you get started.

It might be a long and slow process, and it will be difficult at times, but that's okay!

If you keep an open mind and are willing to learn new things, take your time with developing your channel content, maintain a positive and open relationship with your audience, and, above all, do something that makes you creatively fulfilled, you are well on your way to becoming one more productive and happy member of this new world of online entrepreneurs.

Collected here for your convenience are all the creator tips.

1. Do something you like—if you're bored, your audience is bored.
2. Continually build and improve upon your skill set.
3. While many channels feature links to their Patreon page on their YouTube channel or video descriptions, this is separate from YouTube. For some channels, YouTube has the "membership" feature available, which functions like Patreon, where audience members can give a certain amount in return for perks, but it is much more limited.
4. The success of your Patreon comes from your audience. If you have no audience, there is no reason to make a Patreon—that alone is no guarantee you will make money
5. While it is a good thing there are more people than ever on YouTube in terms of the chances of getting eyes on your content, there is also a disadvantage. Mike Falzone says, "The way it was explained to me by someone who worked at YouTube was [YouTube] used to be like a town, and so it's easy to get recognized in your town. You do good work, and then the town talks about it. And then it became a city...and now it's a world. There's a lot of people on the website but it's significantly harder to break

through." But that doesn't mean you shouldn't try if this is what you want to do.

6. Make good stuff first.

7. As other ways of making money, many YouTubers write books, both fiction and nonfiction, expressing themselves creatively by sharing their experiences in essays or writing about something else altogether. Musicians may also sell their recordings, albums, or arrangements. There is also the ever-popular merchandising of a creator's brand. Many creators sell merchandise (often shortened to just "merch") that can range from anything to t-shirts and hats to buttons and stickers. These usually feature the logo or name of the creator as well as inside jokes and references to the content itself for fans who may be strangers in real life to identify each other.

8. On being a YouTuber, Matt Cremona says, "If someone says it's easy, they're lying to you." But "it's incredibly rewarding and fun and I couldn't imagine doing anything else."

9. If you like instant gratification or feedback, Patreon is a good place to release content as soon as you are finished.

10. When you get hundreds or thousands of comments, it can be time-consuming to go through all of them. But taking some time, maybe even setting a time

limit, and replying to some comments can go a long way to show your audience just how much you care.

11. Chris Christian discovered that an audience will "follow you anywhere...and they'll watch you or listen to you talk about anything." You just need to earn it.

12. Consider what the impact of your content could be. Will it inspire a movement? Breathe life into a dead fandom? Just make people happy?

13. While talking to fellow YouTuber Philip DeFranco, Sean Evans reflected, "We're very fortunate in that the success that we have, we're creatively fulfilled by it. And then the failures that we have, it's the same exact way. I'm not necessarily working and doing something for other people and not feeling interested or emotionally involved. That, to me, is what I hold on to and treasure most."

14. Treat your project as seriously as you want to—but always remember to keep fun at the core!

15. Since YouTube is a visual medium, keep in mind the importance of not just the content of the videos, but the thumbnails themselves. A personal brand encompasses not just the content and format of the videos; it could also include the thumbnails and titles. You could have a little symbol, like Val Carias's spyglass, or a certain way of wording your titles. If we go back to Sean Evans and *Hot Ones* for

a minute, those titles include the interviewee name and a present-tense action relating to the episode, such as "Key & Peele Lose Their Minds Eating Spicy Wings." Don't underestimate thumbnails, either, in driving traffic to your video. Videos might include clickbait phrases or pictures in the thumbnails, while the titles might seem neutral. I see many theory videos use arrows and circles to give a quick preview of the content—and it has worked on me and thousands of others. Yes, creating thumbnails might include learning some new skills, or you can farm it out to a freelance graphic designer. Just something to think about.

16. Several videos for my project were simply list videos, a popular video format in the same way listicles are a popular blog format. It's a simple way to organize many thoughts, and if the video is "counting down" to the number one whatever, that is another great way to keep audience eyes on the video until the very end.

17. Do your research!

18. Val Carias says, "Make sure of what you're getting into. Make sure it's what you want to do, because it's a very tough job, 24/7...And it can get difficult at times...it can get lonely. So again, have friends who are doing the same with you...Always try to remember what kind of person you are and try to

tailor your channel to that type of person...And then always ask yourself what do you want your audience to feel? That's a good question to answer before you make a video."

19. Find something you are passionate about and share it!

20. Editing can be the longest part of the video creation process, even if you have a strategy to get through the raw footage like I do. If I have an hour of raw footage, I'm looking at around three+ hours of editing. Adding extras like subtitles, overlays, pictures, and music can take even longer. What I'm trying to say here is...plan ahead. If you think it takes a long time to film something, try editing!

21. Some YouTubers have a second channel where they might put more personal or behind-the-scenes content. In some cases, it seems like a leftover from the days before Patreon when you wanted your primary channel to be clean with just your final product and only your most dedicated fans would bother subscribing to your second channel. I've noticed more and more "second channels" I subscribed to have been used less and less lately. It could also be a personal or branding choice, where you want to make content that you feel does not belong on your main channel. Starting out, you probably don't need a second channel.

22. Take breaks from social media on occasion! It does everyone a world of good to get away, but even more so when you have constant interactions with an audience. Tell your followers you will be taking a break, then do. If you want a clean break, go for a month. But I have also seen people take the weekends to reconnect with the "real-time world."
23. Just do it! You can't get any feedback if you don't publish anything.
24. Consider starting a second business venture separate from your primary project down the road, especially if creative burnout sets in.
25. If you want to create a catchphrase, go for it! Don't force it, and keep it simple and easy to say. Many YouTubers do end up having catchphrases, as well as a special name for their audience members, much like a regular book/movie fandom, to complete the brand that goes along with their channel name and concept. Focus on the content first, and as you build your audience, your brand will fall into place.
26. It will be HARD to transition to being a full-time creator, harder than you might think, especially in terms of motivation. Find ways to keep yourself accountable. From past school and work experience, you should know what works for you.
27. Strive for improvement, not perfection.

28. Purely wanting to make something and share it can lead to consistency and spending more time as a creator.

29. If you choose a weekly schedule and you're afraid you will end up in a rut, keep a running list of video ideas, whether they are internet challenges—though successful challenge videos need to keep timing in mind—or a broad topic or scraps of a script.

30. Jenna Marbles says, "Be yourself. Figure out what your voice is and use it. Say it, and unapologetically be yourself. But also engage with people. So if you're problematic and someone's like, "Hey, you're being really problematic," then take that advice. Understand what constructive criticism is."

31. Never expect to get big.

32. The cool thing about technology is creators do not have to be in the same room to collaborate. They can record things separately, or if it is more of a conversation, record the conversation itself, like a video chat. But it is easy to tell when creators are in the same room and they are just enjoying each other's creative spirits, or they are bouncing off each other's humor. Collaboration can be fun! Collaboration does not just have to occur between creators in the same field, like two musicians, comedians, or fandom experts. Two creators from different "genres" can collaborate as a means of cross-promotion.

For example, someone who writes or covers music could collaborate with someone who does makeup or other tutorials that require background music.

33. View others in your field not as competitors but as peers and potential collaborators.

34. It will take time to find your creative voice in this new medium, so practice.

35. Hannah Hart says, "The more self-knowledge, self-acceptance, and approval you can give to yourself as a creative, the better experience you're going to have. I'm not looking to be the number one YouTuber or the number one anything. I'm looking to maintain my creative career. So any day that I wake up and I still get a chance to do this? That's a good day."

36. Safety first! Be smart with what you choose to share online. Never post your phone number, your address, or personal email address. Create an email account just for your audience. Open a P.O. box so your audience can send you things. Keep identifying street signs and window views out of your shots. Do not reveal where you work (if YouTube is not yet your full-time job). Once you post something online, it is up there forever, and if audience members want to find you, they will find a way. Be careful, be smart, and report any harassment.

Sources

Intro:

Wayne, Nathaniel in discussion with the author, January 31, 2019.

"YouTube for Press." YouTube. (August 18, 2019).

Part 1 Intro:

Dickey, Megan. "The 22 Key Turning Points in the History of You-Tube." *Business Insider.* February 15, 2013.

Chapter 1:

"Algorithm." *Merriam-Webster.* (August 18, 2019).

Business Insider. "How Hank Green became one of the Internet's most influential educators." YouTube video, 2:57. Posted [March 2015].

Ohlheiser, Abby. "It's 2018, and Hank Green still believes the Internet can make the world better." *The Washington Post.* June 24, 2018.

"Troll." *Merriam-Webster.* (August 18, 2019).

"What is fair use?" *YouTube.* (August 18, 2019).

Chapter 2:

Chaykowski, Kathleen. "Digital Medici: How This Musician-Turned-Entrepreneur Plans to Save Creators From Advertising." *Forbes.* February 13, 2018.

Conte, Jack. "Pedals Music Video (featuring REAL robots)—Conte." YouTube video, 6:08. Posted [May 2013].

"How Much do YouTubers Make?—A YouTuber's Pocket Guide [Calculator]." *Influencer Marketing Hub.* May 16, 2019.

JackConteExtras. "Pedals Behind the Scenes." YouTube video, 9:02. Posted [May 2013].

Kafka, Peter. "Full transcript: Patreon founder and CEO Jack Conte on Recode Media." *Vox.* August 22, 2017.

"Millions and Billions: Celebrating Patrons, Creators, and Major Milestones." *Patreon Blog.* January 23, 2019.

"YouTube elevates most popular users to partners." *YouTube Blog*. May 3, 2007.

Chapter 3:

Cremona, Matt in discussion with the author, January 21, 2019.

Falzone, Mike in discussion with the author, January 25, 2019.

Perez, Sarah. "YouTube introduces channel memberships, merchandise and premieres." *Tech Crunch*. June 21, 2018.

Triton Tools. "Matt Cremona making a Windsor chair from fresh logs." YouTube video, 14:59. Posted [October 2017].

"What is a YouTube MCN?" *Media Kix*. February 15, 2016.

Chapter 4:

Christian, Chris in discussion with the author, January 21, 2019.

Cook, James. "Twitch founder: we turned a 'terrible idea' into a billion-dollar company." *Business Insider*. October 20, 2014.

Mior, Lisa. "The past, present and future of Twitch: an interview with Chase from Twitch.tv." *CG Mag Online*. September 7, 2018.

Garun, Natt. "YouTube launches Super Chat, a tool that lets you pay to pin comments on live streams." *The Verge*. January 12, 2017.

Smith, Dominic in discussion with the author, January 28, 2019.

SmokeScreen. "Game of Thrones Season 7 Episode 7 Finale Review / Reaction—Live Charity Show!" YouTube video, 4:03:26. Posted [August 2017].

"Support St. Jude Children's Hospital!" *Tiltify*. (August 19, 2019).

"We'll do it live—a new chapter in YouTube's live stream." *YouTube Creator Blog*. June 23, 2016.

Chapter 5:

BUILD Series. "Sean Evans Speaks On His Show 'Hot Ones.'" YouTube video, 22:08. Posted [June 2017].

DeFranco, Philip. "A Conversation With Ep 2—Sean Evans Reveals How He Truly Feels About Hot Ones, Kevin Hart, & More!" YouTube video, 56:37. Posted [April 2018].

First We Feast. "The Jonas Brothers Burn Up While Eating Spicy Wings | Hot Ones." YouTube video, 27:30. Posted [May 2019].

Smith, Dave. "Inside the hottest show on YouTube, where celebrities answer questions while eating blazing hot wings." *Business Insider.* November 29, 2017.

Chapter 6:

Abbey, Alison. "The Best Parts of Rhett & Link, Plus an Exclusive Interview With the Internet's Kings of Comedy." *Parade.* May 19, 2017.

Ifeanyi, KC. "Inside The "Mythical" Minds And Digital Empire Of YouTube Pioneers Rhett & Link." *Fast Company.* March 29, 2017.

Chapter 7:

Because Geek. "FULL ANALYSIS of leaked Kit Harington on set picture - Game of Thrones S06 News." YouTube video, 7:26. Posted [September 2015].

Because Geek. "Game of Thrones Season 6 - The Proud Lord's Dead - Stark Revenge." YouTube video, 25:44. Posted [April 2016].

Carias, Val in discussion with the author, January 24, 2019.

First We Feast. "Key & Peele Lose Their Minds Eating Spicy Wings | Hot Ones." YouTube video, 14:10. Posted [April 2016].

Chapter 8:

Binging with Babish. "Binging with Babish 1 Million Subscriber Special: Taco Town & Behind the Scenes." YouTube video, 8:38. Posted [July 2017].

"Binging with Babish's Andrew Rea on the Secret to his Success." *Milk Street*. November 20, 2018.

Maher, Michael. "Interview: Behind the Scenes with YouTube's Binging with Babish." *Premium Beat*. July 18, 2017.

Margine, Claire. "The Creator Behind "Binging with Babish" Goes to Sleep Watching YouTube." *The Kitchn*. July 26, 2018.

Chapter 9:

Drew's Corner—Drew C. Ryan. "MALINDA KATHLEEN REESE (GOOGLE TRANSLATE SINGS) INTERVIEW—Reel Geek Girls #70." YouTube video, 9:24. Posted [November 2017].

Lara6683. "Mega Medley that was supposed to be 5 minutes but wasn't." YouTube video, 1:25:12. Posted [November 2017].

"Malinda Kathleen Reese Extended Interview." *Mixcloud*. Podcast, 25:01. Posted [November 2015].

Translator Fails. "Google Translate Sings: "Wrecking Ball" by Miley Cyrus (PARODY)." YouTube video, 4:56. Posted [June 2014].

Translator Fails. "Google Translate Sings: You'll Be Back from Hamilton." YouTube video, 5:02. Posted [September 2016].

Translator Fails. "'Let It Go' from Frozen according to Google Translate (PARODY)." YouTube video, 4:29. Posted [February 2014].

Chapter 10:

Emily. "Catching up with the Super Carlin Brothers: YouTube, Theories, Fandom, and More!" *Nerds and Beyond.* April 17, 2018.

Melcon, Andrew. "Discord: Everything You Need to Know." *Tom's Guide.* March 11, 2018.

SuperCarlinBrothers. "THE BIG ANNOUNCEMENT!" YouTube video, 4:34. Posted [September 2018].

SuperCarlinBrothers. "The Pixar Theory." YouTube video, 12:08. Posted [July 2013].

Chapter 11:

Martin, Ian in discussion with the author, January 29, 2019.

Chapter 12:

Cannell, Sean. "Why Consistency is the Key to Growing your You-
Tube Channel." *LinkedIn*. October 16, 2018.

JennaMarbles. "My Dogs Draw Their Lives." YouTube video, 4:31.
Posted [July 2015].

JennaMarbles. "Prank Calling In Sick From Jobs I Don't Have." You-
Tube video, 10:36. Posted [September 2015].

JennaMarbles. "Putting 200 Fake Nails On One Nail." YouTube video,
13:37. Posted [March 2018].

Patel, Deep. "YouTube Superstar Jenna Marbles Reveals the Secrets
to Her Success." *HuffPost*. April 10, 2017.

SRU Rocket. "An Interview with Jenna Marbles." YouTube video, 5:55.
Posted [September 2018].

Chapter 13:

Wayne, Nathaniel in discussion with the author, January 31, 2019.

Chapter 14:

HOLLENS CREATOR ACADEMY. "How to Make a Living Online
- Peter Hollens." YouTube video, 5:18. Posted [December 2017].

Potts, Ricky. "Artist Interview: 1-on-1 with Peter Hollens." *Ricky Lee Potts*. June 2017.

Ross, Danny. "How Peter Hollens Changed the Music Industry From His Living Room." *Forbes*. March 8, 2017.

Zellner, Xander. "Peter Hollens, A Cappella Breakout Star, Talks First Chart-Topping Album *Legendary Folk Songs*." *Billboard*. June 29, 2018.

Chapter 15:

Ellis, Lindsay. "That Time Disney Remade Beauty and the Beast." YouTube video, 36:52. Posted [July 2018].

Ellis, Lindsay. "The Hobbit: The Desolation of Warners (Part 3/2)." YouTube video, 30:37. Posted [April 2018].

Graham, Kathryn. "Kathryn Graham has a Conversation with Lindsay Ellis—Part I." *TV Writer*. January 9, 2019.

Graham, Kathryn. "A Conversation with Lindsay Ellis—Part II." *TV Writer*. January 16, 2019.

Chapter 16:

MyHarto. "My Drunk Kitchen Ep. 1: Butter Yo Shit." YouTube video, 5:21. Posted [March 2011].

Saxe, Lizzy. "How Do You Describe Hannah Hart's Career? It's Complicated." *Forbes.* November 28, 2018.

Tiffany, Kaitlyn. "My Drunk Kitchen creator Hannah Hart on life as a YouTube star." *The Verge.* October 19, 2016.

Acknowledgements

For as long as I can remember, I've wanted to publish a book. In less than a year's time, I've gone from being just another person with a curiosity, a penchant for research, and a love of writing — I am now a published author. Throughout this journey, I have found book publishing to be a very collaborative process. There is no way I could have finished and published *Fulfilled, not Famous* without support from so many people.

First and foremost, thank you to my family: Mom, Dad, Daniel, and David. You've all helped out in one way or another throughout this entire journey (special shout-out to Mom who was my first advanced reader!). I appreciate how you helped me keep the book a secret for several months and thanks for putting up with me during my multiple-hour editing sessions!

Thank you to all my other family members who preordered multiple copies of my book and spread it around social media: G & G Rathburn, U Steve & Kristen, G & G Prichard, A Jen & U Tom, U Scott & A Kerry, and U Jeff & U Steve. Without your love and support I would not have reached my campaign goal.

Thank you to my oldest and dearest friends: Tyler Fuller, Rosie Pregler, and Clare Weisenfluh. Our years of random creative shenanigans put me on the path that got me here and your cheerleading throughout this process has been invaluable.

Thank you to New Degree Press, my multiple editors, Brian Bies, and Professor Eric Koester, who were with me each step of the way of turning a vague idea into a whole book.

Finally, thank you to everyone else who pre-ordered a book, donated to the publishing costs, gave me time for an interview, read my draft, gave input on my cover, spread the word, and offered support in any other way. Whether you are friends, extended family, co-workers, professors, or complete strangers, I am very sincerely grateful for your help in making this dream a reality.

Eric Koester	Jonathan R. Moser	Loren & Linda Prichard***
Tom & Jennifer Clark***	Frank & Jane Pregler***	Sherrie Flick
George & Judy Rathburn***	Rose Pregler	Rachel Troychock
Jeffrey Prichard & Stephen Kanouse***	Michael Miele	Christian Goulione
Nathan Nitczynski	Erin Skelly	Jeanette Fournier
Scott & Kerry Prichard	Linda Federici	Deborah Morvay
Clare Weisenfluh	Scott & Jill Rathburn***	Donald & Shirley Flick
Martha Schimp	Kyle Sliker	Melanie Zajac
Lois Sliker	Dona McWilliams	Bob & Rose Rathburn
Ed Curtin	Stacy Langer	Jordan Mushrush
Steve Rathburn & Kristen Taccone	Justin Ross	Laura DiFranco
Mike Falzone ~	Dominic Smith ~	Chris Christian ~
Matt Cremona ~	Val Carias ~	Ian Martin ~
Nathaniel Wayne ~		

***   purchased more than one copy

~   featured interviewee